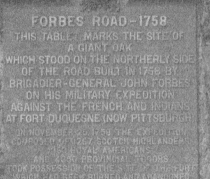

FORBES ROAD—1758
THIS TABLET MARKS THE SITE OF
A GIANT OAK
WHICH STOOD ON THE NORTHERLY SIDE
OF THE ROAD BUILT IN 1758 BY
BRIGADIER-GENERAL JOHN FORBES
ON HIS MILITARY EXPEDITION
AGAINST THE FRENCH AND INDIANS
AT FORT DUQUESNE (NOW PITTSBURGH)

ON NOVEMBER 25, 1758 THE EXPEDITION
COMPOSED OF 1267 SCOTCH HIGHLANDER
1953 ROYAL AMERICANS
AND 4050 PROVINCIAL TROOPS
TOOK POSSESSION OF THE SITE OF THE FORT
WHICH HAD BEEN BURNED AND ABANDONED
THE NIGHT BEFORE
THIS ACHIEVEMENT RESULTED
IN THE PERMANENT OCCUPATION OF
THE ADJACENT TERRITORY
BY ENGLISH-SPEAKING PEOPLE
ERECTED BY THE PENNSYLVANIA SOCIETY
COLONIAL DAMES OF AMERICA
1914

LETTERS
of
GENERAL JOHN FORBES
relating to the
EXPEDITION AGAINST FORT DUQUESNE
IN 1758

Compiled from Books in the
Carnegie Library of Pittsburgh

for the

Allegheny County Committee
Pennsylvania Society

of the

Colonial Dames of America

by

Irene Stewart
Reference Librarian, Carnegie Library of Pittsburgh

To which is added a list of
References on the Expedition

Pittsburgh
Allegheny County Committee
1927

The letters from "Correspondence of William Pitt with Colonial Governors in America" are here reprinted with the courteous permission of The MacMillan Company; those from the Pennsylvania Magazine of History and Biography, through the courtesy of the Historical Society of Pennsylvania.

FOREWORD

The Allegheny County Committee feels that in placing these letters before the public they are rendering a service peculiarly fitting to the people of Pennsylvania. Around Fort Duquesne centered the struggle between the French and the English for supremacy in the country west of the Alleghanies. This struggle ended in the victory of General John Forbes, who wrested Fort Duquesne from the French and gave to it the name of Pittsburgh, in honor of William Pitt, Prime Minister of England.

Helen H. Pearson, *Chairman of the Allegheny County Committee.*

March 28, 1927.

INTRODUCTION

The expedition against Fort Duquesne in 1758 was one of the three campaigns of that year by which William Pitt, then in full control of foreign and military affairs in England, hoped to overpower the French forces in America. Of the other two campaigns the one against Louisbourg was successful and the town was taken by the British under Amherst in July. In the same month, however, the English forces under Abercrombie were repulsed with great loss in the campaign against Ticonderoga and Crown Point.

General John Forbes, who was placed in command of the campaign against Fort Duquesne, was a Scotch soldier born in 1710, son of Colonel John Forbes of Pittencrieff, county Fife. He was sent to America in 1757 as adjutant-general, and in December of the same year was appointed brigadier-general. Preparations for the campaign against the French on the Ohio were soon begun. Forbes reached Philadelphia in April, where he was compelled to wait for troops and supplies until the last of June. He then set out and by slow and difficult stages marched toward Fort Duquesne. Although he had at first intended to lead his army by Braddock's road, he changed his plan and decided upon a more direct route, opening, from Bedford, a new road over the mountains. This decision was not carried out without much opposition from the Virginians, headed by Colonel Washington, and the controversy that arose (fully discussed in Hulbert's "Old Glade Road") is one of the most interesting incidents of the campaign.

General Forbes had, in the meantime, been stricken with an illness from which he never recovered. He was carried over the mountains in a litter, suffering greatly from pain and weakness, yet he directed in person almost every detail of the campaign, facing with resolute courage the difficulties that presented themselves at every turn. The new road was rendered almost impassable by unusually heavy rains, and had continually to be repaired; supplies were hard to procure in sufficient quantities; the horses were overworked and starving. Winter was approaching, and early in November, upon reaching Loyalhanna, Forbes decided to go into winter quarters there and to resume operations in the spring. He learned, however, from prisoners that were brought in that the French were almost without defense and could not withstand an attack. He then decided to advance, and upon approaching the fort found that the French, deserted by their Indian allies through the efforts of Frederick Post, and cut off from their base of supplies by the surrender of Fort Frontenac, had blown up the fort and fled. Forbes immediately took possession of the place and built a rough stockade in which he left a small portion of his troops.

Early in December he set out on his return. Unable to ride, he was carried in his litter the entire distance to Philadelphia, where he died on the tenth of March. He was buried with military honors in Christ Church.

The following extract from Forbes's letter to Pitt contains the short sentence which records the naming of Pittsburgh, and shows in what spirit and with what hopes the name was given to the site of the ruined fort.

Pittsbourgh. 27th Novemr. 1758.

Sir,

I do myself the Honour of acquainting you that it has pleased God to crown His Majesty's Arms with Success over all His Enemies upon the Ohio, by my having obliged the Enemy to burn and abandon Fort Du Quesne, which they effectuated on the 25th:, and of which I took possession next day, the Enemy having made their Escape down the River towards the Missisippi in their Boats, being abandoned by their Indians, whom I had previously engaged to leave them, and who now seem all willing and ready to implore His Majesty's most Gracious Protection. So give me leave to congratulate you upon this great Event, of having totally expelled the French from this prodigious tract of Country, and of having reconciled the various tribes of Indians inhabiting it to His Majesty's Government.

* * * * * * * * * *

This far I had wrote at Fort Du Quesne upon the 27th: Novemr. since which time I have never, either been able to write, or capable to dictate a letter.

* * * * * * * * * *

I have used the freedom of giving your name to Fort Du Quesne, as I hope it was in some measure the being actuated by your spirits that now makes us Masters of the place. Nor could I help using the same freedom in the naming of two other Forts that I built (Plans of which I send you) the one Fort Ligonier & the other Bedford. I hope the name Fathers will take them under their Protection, In which case these dreary deserts will soon be the richest and most fertile of any possest by the British in No. America. I have the honour to be with great regard and Esteem Sir,

Your most obed.t. & most humle. servt.

Jo: Forbes.

Philadelphia. 21st January 1759.

The principal sources of information on the campaign are the Bouquet papers, in the British Museum, and the official correspondence of Forbes, preserved in the British Public Record Office. The letters here reproduced are those which are available in the Carnegie Library of Pittsburgh. Though but a small part of Forbes's correspondence, these letters, chiefly to William Pitt, Governor Denny of Pennsylvania and Governor Sharpe of Maryland, form a valuable history of this difficult and important campaign. A very few letters not by General Forbes have been included because of their relevancy and for the sake of continuity. Aside from their value as an authentic record of the campaign, they have an interest because of the light they throw upon the strongly marked personal qualities and characteristics of the writer, of whose life we have only the most meagre sketches. We have a number of excellent accounts of this expedition, but it is only by reading the letters themselves that one can at all grasp the hardships that had to be endured and the difficulties of every kind that had to be overcome.

LETTERS OF GENERAL FORBES
To Governor Denny
Pennsylvania Colonial records, v.8, p.59

Sir:

I have the favour of yours of the 17th, and make no manner of doubt of your doing of every thing in your Power in forwarding His Majesty's Service, and therefore must beg that the Officers and Soldiers raised in Pennsylvania for the Service are Able Bodied good Men, capable of enduring fatigue, and that their Arms be the best that can be found in the Province; As Carpenters and Axe Men are absolutely necessary upon Many Occasions, I must recommend the sending as many of those as can be conveniently got into the Troops.

And likewise that the Province will raise fifty good Men, well mounted upon light Serviceable Horses, and every way accoutred to serve in conjunction with those to be furnished by the other Provinces as a Body of Light Horse, from whom I expect very Important Service.

As the Roads from Lancaster to Williams' Ferry upon the Potomack may want considerable repairs and widening of them for the Carriages of Cannon, &cᵃ., I have therefore wrote to the Governor of Maryland for that Purpose, In order that those roads may be repaired by the Inhabitants of the 2 Provinces of Pennsylvania and Maryland, living near those parts.

As I propose Assembling the Regular Troops, and those of Pennsylvania, at Conegochieque, about the 20th of April; You will therefore give Orders for all Manner of Diligence to be used in raising the Numbers that your Province is to send, who shall be payed at the rate of 4 pence p Diem, in lieu of provisions from the time they begin their March; until that they are furnished with Provisions from the King's Stores.

I am informed that the Inhabitants upon the Frontiers of your Province being much used to hunting in the Woods, would consequently make good Rangers, In which case I am to beg you will give your direction for the forming some of your properest Men into Companys of Rangers with good Officers, who are well acquainted with the Country, to Command them.

If it could possibly be contrived to find some Intelligent Person who would venture up to the Ohio, either as a Merchant or a Deserter, & would bring us Intelligence what was going on in those parts, I should certainly reward him handsomely. Perhaps such a one might be found in some of your Provincial Companies up at Fort Loudoun, &c^a., &c^a.

I should be obliged to you if you will give orders to send me some Account of what provincial Troops you have now on Foot, and where they are for the present, as likewise what Numbers (in the whole) your Province is to raise for the Service of the present Year.

I must beg the favour that you will Order your Secretary to send the Inclosed Packett by an Express to Virginia, And I shall have the Honour to be with great regard, Sir,

Your Most Obedient & most humble Servant,

Jo. Fforbes.

New York, March 20th, 1758.

P. S.—I have this moment an Express from Fort Edward, acquainting me of One of your Scouting Parties of 180 Men having been attacked by a Thousand of the Enemy's Indians, Canadians, &c^a., near Ticonderoga, in which we have lost 130 Men; the Party behaved most Gallantly, but were overpowered by Numbers.

To Governor Dobbs

Colonial records of North Carolina, v.5, p.926

New York, 21st March 1758.

Sir,

His Excellency Maj^r Genl Abercromby having pursuant to his Majesty's Directions been appointed unto the Command of the Kings regular Forces and Provincial troops, who are to be employed jointly in the operations to be carried on this ensuing Campaign to the southward of Pensylvania included,

And as a great part of this force is to consist of the Southern Provincial troops of Pensilvania, Maryland, Virginia and North Carolina, I make no manner of doubt but these Provinces from their known Zeal for the publick service will most chearfully and unanimously join in raising with the greatest Dispatch the Body of Men expected from them for the Defence of their own Confines and the Honour and support of his Majesty's Dominions in N^o America,

I must therefore beg that the officers and men employed for this Service be able bodied good men, capable of enduring fatigue, and that their arms be the best that can be found in the Province.

As I am given to understand and have great reason to expect that a Body of Cherokee Indians are to come and join us this Spring on the back Frontiers of Virginia and Pensilvania, and as their Rout leads them through your Province of North Carolina, I must therefore beg that you will be so good as to give orders that they meet with all kind of good usage in their passing, and hope that Mr. Atkins who has the Charge of Indian Affairs has taken Care of their being supplied with Provisions &c. upon their March. As I am a Stranger to the Southern Provinces, and therefore can make no guess of the Distance that the N⁰ Carolina troops will have to march in order to join the Army at Wills⁸ Creek upon the Potowmack by the first of May, you will therefore be so good as to regulate their march, and order them to set out so as they may join me by that time. And as Provisions cannot possibly be delivered to them upon their march, each effective man that joins the Army shall be paid four pence sterling in lieu of Provisions from the time he begins his march, until that he receives Provisions from the Stores.

I must beg Sir that you will give your orders that none but those men who are good and that can be depended upon may be sent, as people either inclined to mutiny or desert wo^d prove an immense Detriment to the service at so intricate a Time, and that you will give orders to send me an account of the men you have at present in pay, and what numbers I may expect you are to send me, with the route they are to take in order to join me, and the time they will be ready to sett out, and you will order the officer that commands them to correspond with me directed for me at Philadelphia.

I have the honour to be with great regard

Your most obedient, &c.,

Jo Forbes.

To Governor Denny
Pennsylvania Colonial records, v.8, p.60

Sir:

As there will be a Number of Waggons and Carriages wanted in the Province of Pennsylvania, and as the Inhabitants may be backward in furnishing of them, altho' to be payed for them with ready Money, I therefore take this Opportunity of letting you know that Press Warrants will be necessary all over the Province, In order that if you are not vested with the Power to grant such Warrants, that you will apply to the Assembly to grant theirs, and fix prices upon the Different Carriages and Horses. I have the Honour to be, Sir,

Your most Obedient and most humble Servant,

Jo. Fforbes.

New York, March 23d.

To Governor Sharpe
Archives of Maryland, v.9, p.167

Sir

I Have the Honour of Yours of the 27th of March, the Contents of which I Communicated to General Abercromby, who Allows me to tell you, that he thinks himself Bound to make good the Obligation that the Earl of Loudoun Entered into, with regard to the Maryland Troops Garrisoned at Fort Cumberland, and cannot Imagine that the Province of Maryland, will, at this Critical time, Allow that Fort to be Abandoned. And makes no doubt but from your prudence & Zeal for the publick Service, that you will be able to persuade the Province, not only to Continue those Troops there, but with all Diligence to second His Majesty's Intentions, in Raising as many more Troops as the Necessity of the present Circumstances and the Strength of the Province will Admit of.

I am Extreamly obliged to you, for the Care you have taken to Repair the Roads, and for your orders about providing of Forrage at Conegocheugue, &c.

Sir Iohn St Clair who left this two days ago, will soon be up in those parts, & has money to Satisfye & pay for what will be Necessary.

I should be glad that any of the Scouting partys were so lucky as to bring a Prisoner from Fort Duquesne, as by that means something might be Learned, & hope the Encouragement you give the Cherokees will keep them alert, & make them Exert themselves in this Service.

As soon as the Troops Destined for the Service in the West Arrives at Philadelphia, I have General Abercromby's orders to send proper Detachments up to Fort Cumberland. I hope soon to set out to Philadelphia, & shall be very happy in paying my Respects to you in Maryland, being with great Regard,

Sir, Y^r most Hum^{ble} and most Ob^t Servt

Jo: fforbes

New York Aprile 4th 1758

To Governor Denny

Pennsylvania Colonial records, v.8, p.79

Philadelphia, April 20th, 1758.

Sir:

As the Situation of these Provinces is such at this Critical Juncture as requires all possible Means to be exerted to clear this Province of the Enemy who have at this Time invaded it, and as there is a great Scarcity of Arms for that purpose, I am under the necessity of requiring of your Honour that you will give orders for delivering to me Two Hundred and Eighteen Light Fuzees, which are in your Store, as likewise as many of the 165 Arms as are found to be serviceable after they are Surveyed.

There will remain in your Store more Arms than will Compleat the Forces proposed to be raised by this Province, besides 2,000 Arms, which I have an Account of being embarked for the Service of this Expedition. I am, with the greatest regard,

Your Honour's most Obedient and most Humble Servant,

Jo. Fforbes.

To Governor Denny
Pennsylvania Colonial records, v.8, p.83

Philadelphia, April 21st, 1758.

Sir:

I am extremely sorry that any just request of mine to you, as first Majestrate, should meet with obstructions that I neither could forsee nor suppose; particularly as I had signed a receipt for the Arms I had demanded, according to your desire; and by which receipt of mine, I certainly showed the Necessity that I was under for such an application, in order to support His Majesty's Measures for the general welfare of North America, and for the immediate protection of this Province in Particular. Such a refusal of what is the Undoubted Right of the King to demand, or the Officer Commanding his Majesty's Subjects under Arms in the Province, is what I am astonished at; and as the Service is pressing, and will admit of no delay, I must beg, Sir, you will send me an answer in writing, as soon as possible, whether you are to deliver to my orders the Fuzees demanded, or not.

I have the Honour to be, with the greatest regard,

Sir, Your most obedient and most hum. Servant,

Jo. Forbes.

To Governor Denny
Pennsylvania Archives, ser. 1, v.3, p.383

Sir,

Accident presented a particular thing to my view this day that had really escaped me, and therefore beg your Advice.

As your troops are immediately under my direction, and as the different demands of money from them is perhaps what neither you nor I can either determine or forsee, And as there may be severall Contingent expences accruing dayly that I can not have your advice in, I must therefore represent to you that it will be necessary that you have a provinciall treasurer or paymaster to attend me, In order to issue such summs of money for the provinciall service as I shall judge necessary to give orders for. It is needless to explain or to enter into the detail of what those demands may be, because every person must easily forsee a number of trifling demands, that at present I can not ascertain, but hope you will fall upon a method to give me such powers that no stop may be putt to the service, as I shall think myself accountable to you and the province for any moneys that may by my orders be laid out.

I am, Sir,
with great regard,
Y^r most ob^t & most
humble Servant,

Jo. Fforbes.

Philadelphia, Aprile 28th.

To William Pitt

Correspondence of William Pitt with colonial governors in America, v.1, p.235

Philadelphia. May 1st, 1758.

Sir

By a Letter that I have just received from Major General Abercromby, I am directed to Correspond with you, and impart to His Majesty's Ministers the Steps that I take, and the Events following thereon, in prosecution to the Command entrusted to my Care, that no Time may be lost in informing His Majesty of the progress of His Affairs in the Southern Collonys.

I received General Abercromby's Commands upon the fourteenth of last Month, ordering me to repair from New York to Philadelphia, and there to endeavour to reconceal Matters between the Governour and Assembly, in order to the passing of a Bill of one hundred thousand pounds for His Majesty's use, and Service of this Campaign. The Bill after various Altercations was at last agreed to, and passed upon the 26th of last Month; and the Provincial Troops were order'd to be augmented to two thousand seven hundred Men. They have just now began to raise their Men by naming their Officers &c^a.: a few days will shew what Success the Recruiting Officers meet with; But everything except fresh Disputes which arise every day, goes on very slowly, but I have and shall do everything in my power to quell them.

The three lower Countys are raising three hundred Men, which I have reason to expect will be soon compleated.

The Province of Maryland have been extremely dilatory in their proceedings, nor do I yet find, that they have come to any Resolution about granting Supplys. At the end of last Year they voted their Troops (consisting of three hundred Men) shou'd be disbanded, by which Fort Cumberland and that back Country must have fallen into the Enemy's Hands. But the Earl of Loudoun gave assurances to Governour Sharpe, that rather than these Men shou'd be disbanded his Lord^p wou'd make good the Expences of keeping them up. In this Situation these Troops have been these four or five Months; and as General Abercromby seems averse at present to have that Expence fall upon the Crown, I can have but very little dependance of Maryland doing any Good for the Service; even altho' they grant Eighty thousand Pounds for His Majesty's Use, twenty five or thirty thousand Pounds of which will be appropriated for their long Sessions of Assembly, and great part of the Remainder consumed in the pay and Arrears due to their Troops.

The Province of Virginia have voted to augment their Troops to two thousand Men, and are to garrison their forts and Frontiers with their Militia. But I doubt much if that Province will be able to raise that Number of Men, altho' they give ten pounds enlisting money. The Regiment that they have on foot amounts at present to eight hundred Men, but I may venture to say, that they will not be able to raise four hundred Men more, and if they shou'd draft their Militia to compleat the two thousand Men, these Men will not stay eight days with us. There is nothing expected from the Carolinas, It was impossible to bring the three Independent Companies of South Carolina this way; as they are stationed at the Forts in the Indian Country at the back of Georgia.

The Regular Forces destined for the Operations upon the frontiers of the Southern Provinces and the Ohio, are thirteen Companys of Montgomery's Highlanders, and four Companys of the first Battalion of the Royal American Regiment. The ten Companys of the former are not yet arrived from South Carolina. The three additional Companys who are in this Province, have one third sick, and the remainder have not yet recovered strength enough for Service, occasioned by their long passage from Britain. The four Companies of the first Battalion of Americans are got to this Place, they are sickly, being just arrived from South Carolina, and they want fifty Men to compleat them, which will be impracticable to fill up, as the Provinces are giving so high Bountys for raising the Men they are to furnish during this Campaign. . . . The Cherokee and Catauba Indians have been fully as good as their Promise, in coming in at different times from their own Country for these two or three Months by past, to Winchester in Virginia, the place of their Rendez-vous. Their Numbers already come, are Six hundred and fifty two, and several more are expected, and are actually upon their March. As they are almost naked, and without Arms, I have left no Means untryed to provide them in both and have so far succeeded that I have now scouting Partys to the Amount of four hundred of them (all equipt for War) who are gone upon the Ohio, above and below Fort Duquesne, in order to annoy the Enemy, gett Intelligence, and bring away some Prisoners if possible. As fast as the rest can be equipt they shall go out upon the same Errand. For as our greatest Dependance is upon them, and they capable of being led away upon any Caprice or whime that seizes them, I am obliged by every Artifice to amuse them from returning home, they being rather offended at not seeing our Army and Artillery assembled, which I am afraid they had reason to expect. However, I propose getting Governour Sharpe and an officer from this to go amongst them to keep up their Spirits, by constant Employment, altho' that may be difficult to do, without equiping them for War; which equipment for one thousand Indians amounts to the Value of Eight thousand Pounds, and many of the things not to be gott in America, especially light Arms.

In the mean time until the Troops arrive from South Carolina, the Artillery and Stores from England, and that the Provincial Forces are raised and collected at their different Rendez-vous: I shall be preparing the Magazines, and moving them up fifty or sixty Miles beyond the inhabited parts of this Province, that no Stop may be made for want of that Material Article provision. . . . I had the Honour of your Letter (dated at Whitehall Janry. the 27th.) the 24th. of last Month, with a Letter for Governour Lyttleton. I executed the Orders it contained by writing directly to Colonel Montgomery I shall take care that he be immediately acquainted with its contents upon his arrival here. . . . I beg leave to assure you that no diligence or application of mine shall ever be wanting to help forward the Service to the utmost of my Power.

I am Sir, with the greatest Regard and Respect
Your most obedient and most humble Servant
Jo: Forbes.

To Governor Sharpe
Archives of Maryland, v.9, p.174

Private   Philadelphia, May 2d 1758.
Sir,

In case your Assembly are mad enough to do Nothing, I like the proposal for the Virginians taking your Troops into their pay extremely, and as I was sending an Express to Mr Blair, I hinted to him that in Case such a proposal was made to him by you, that he ought to Jump at it Directly

But in case he thinks they will be able to Raise their own men, rather than let your Troops be Disbanded, I will take them into the pay of the Crown, upon the Footing of Rangers. And that no time may be lost in Adjusting & Settling those & other measures, I have sent Sir John St Clair to Lancaster, & from thence he is to Repair to Winchester in Virginia, where I have Desired Mr Blair, or some Person, with full powers, to meet him on the 18th of this month, and where also I must beg (if it any way suits your Conveniency) that you will be likewise, as by such a meeting numberless Difficultys may Easily be Removed.

I am, with the greatest Sincerity
Sir,
Your most obedient and
most Humble Servt
Jo: fforbes

To Governor Sharpe
Archives of Maryland, v.9, p.175

Philadelphia May 2d 1758

Sir

I have the Honour of yours of the 27th of April yesterday morning, but as I could not by any means interfere with the Embargo: I sent your Letter with the Memorial to General Abercromby by an Express, and make no doubt, but by the Return of the Express I shall have the pleasure to acquaint you, of the Embargo being taken off; as I hear that all our Troops and Transports are sailed from New York.

I am extremely sorry that the annimositys betwixt your upper and lower House shou'd prove of so fatal a consequence, as to obstruct the Kings measures at this so critical a time for the whole Continent of North America. Can the Gentlemen that compose these Houses, imagine that His Majesty and the whole people of Great Britain will be blind to their Behaviour upon this so urgent and pressing an occasion. And can they imagine that a great nation drained to the last in the protection and Defence of those Provinces and Collonys will forgive and forgett the being abandoned by any of them, in this critical time of publick Calamity and distress: If every individual was honestly to examine his own Heart, I am perswaded he wou'd be stung with a just and laudable Spirit of resentment, at the proceedings of the collected Representatives of the People of Maryland. For my own part I shall be very much difficulted, how I ought to behave my self, if the Province of Maryland does not (in consequence of His Majestys Pleasure communicated to them in the strongest manner by Mr Pitt His Majestys Principal Secretary of State) come to a speedy determination, as one days delay is of infinite consequence. I shall be sorry to let it enter my thoughts, that they are not, to act as good and Loyall Subjects ought to do, because it wou'd grieve me much to think we had ever cherished and protected concealed Ennemys, infinitely more dangerous than the most open and declared ones.

I must beg you will let me know, as soon as possible the Resolutions concluded upon, that I may govern myself accordingly, and believe me to be with great Regard

Sir
Your most obedient and
most humble Servant
Jo. fforbes.

To Governor Denny
Pennsylvania Colonial records, v.8, p.110

Sir:

Finding that the Storeship with the Tents, Arms, &ca., has not arrived from England with the Transports, I applied to General Abercrombie, to know how I was to proceed with regard to Camp Necessaries, and his answer is:

"With regard to Camp necessaries for the Provincials, they must be furnish'd by the different Provinces; those to the Northward have agreed to it, and their Troops are to come provided with them at their Expence." I must therefore beg leave to Know the Resolution of the Province upon this Subject directly.

Upon your Application, I promised to send an Hundred of the Royal Americans up towards Reading, but as these Companies are very Sickly, coming from Carolina, and very much want some Days of Rest and Refreshment, I must, therefore, beg you will excuse me from my Promise, and in their Room you may send some of the new raised Provincials, which will answer every purpose fully as well.

I should be glad to know your Opinion of the Party of Cherokees at Carlisle, whether they should be allowed to proceed, or turned another Way. I should likewise want to know how far the Province thinks themselves Obliged to take Care of those Indians by Presents, Cloathing, &c^a.

I beg, Sir, that the Orders about the Light Horse may be given as soon as possible; And that you will likewise be so good as to order the Horses to be placed, for the Conveying Intelligence thro' your Counties, according to the plan given to you by the Quartermaster General.

I really think Teedyuscung's Demands ought to be agreed with, as he has the Publick Faith for the making such a Settlement, altho' I would parry off all Convoy of Troops, as Axmen and Carpenters will Answer all his purposes, and I think that he and his Tribes ought to be our Guards for those Back Settlements this Summer, as we shall want all the Troops somewhere else.

I am, Sir, with great Regard, Your Most Obedient & most Hum. Servt.

John Forbes.

Philadelphia, May 3d, 1758.

To Governor Sharpe
Archives of Maryland, v.9, p.176

Philadelphia May 12th [1758]

Sir

I had the favour of yours of the 6th and I am sorry to find that your Assembly are so late, in determining, what I believe none but themselves would have either deliberate upon, or have hesitate one moment, in complying with the just and equitable demands of their King and Country.

I understand that Sir Jno St Clair has left Lancaster in order to go and meet you at Fort Frederick or Winchester where I have wrote to Mr Blair of Virginia to come likewise in order to settle the different demands that the provinces may have with regard to Arms Tents &c. that by some mistake or other, are not come from England as was expected. So if your 300 men are to be continued by your Assembly you will be so good as order the necessarys for them and let me know what arms you can spare in your province, as wee shall have great occasion for them, and let them be immediately putt in order.

I must likewise desire that you will order all your troops up to Fort Cumberland and make Colonel Washingtons people take up their post at Fort Frederick &c.

I hope to be able to leave this in a fortnight when I shall be glad to have the pleasure of waiting upon you being with great regard

Sir Y^r most hum & most

ob^t Servt

Jo: fforbes

To William Pitt

Correspondence of William Pitt with colonial governors in America, v.1, p.245

Philadelphia. May 19th.. 1758.

Sir

I did myself the Honour of writing to you the first of this Month giving you a state of the Millitary. affairs in the Southern Provinces at that time. There has little occurred since only I find that this Province begins to complain that the £100,000 voted for the Service of the Year is mostly expended already, owing to one half of that same being appropriated to clear the Arrears due to their Troops and other demands by which in reality they have only given £50,000 for the Service of this Year.

The striking of their Paper Money has taken up so much time that they had not got £10,000 five days ago. So you see Sir those tardy Proceedings will greatly distress our active operations; however I am still in hopes of getting about 1000 of their Men together (including those that they had on foot) by the 1st. of June; But when the rest will be got I can scarce form any Judgement.

The Maryland Assembly have as yet come to no determination, and are in the same situation that I had the honour to acquaint you off, but from some quickening letters that I have lately wrote to that Province I flatter myself they will at least keep the 300 Men now on their pay for this Season and more I scarcely can expect.

The Virginians are going on slowly in compleating their Quota to the 2000 Men that they have agreed to raise, and I shall be well pleased if I get a few more than half their Number by the 1st. of June. Colonel Montgomery's Battalion is not yet come from Carolina, altho' by the last Account I have reason to believe they may be embarking there by this time.

I have therefore marched the three additional Companies of that Battalion, and the 4 Companys of Colo. Stanwix's Battalion into the Back Country, to protect the frontiers until Colo. Montgomery's Battalion arrive, and the new Levies come in.

I am sorry to acquaint you that the Cherokee Indians who have been out upon several scouting party's, and with some Success, begin to weary, and languish after their own homes, complaining that they see no appearance of our Army.

Hitherto I have had the good fortune to amuse them, and keep them from returning, by promises, and presents, but how long I shall be able to continue them with us I cannot say.

But as they are by far the greatest body of Indians that we have ever had to join us, (they being above 700 Men) I thought it my duty to do everything in my power to continue them with us. For which reason I was obliged to purchase the necessarys for equipping of them for Warr, and for presents to them, through this, and all the other Colonies, where such goods and Arms, were to be found. I did imagine that I shou'd have had the Assistance of Sir William Johnston, and of Mr. Atkins in the Manadgement of those Indians, Being informed that those Gentlemen are solely to superintend Indian Affairs, exclusive of any other Person.

But as Sr. William continued at his Settlement 500 Miles North of this, and Mr. Atkins remained at Charlestown 100 Miles to the South, I found myself obliged either to act as I have done or must have seen those Indians return to their own Country disgusted, and probably ready to join the Enemy against us. And even notwithstanding the dilligence I have used in amassing those Goods, there is one Warrior and thirty of his tribe have left us, and another Warriour was actually sett out upon his return, but by sending some Intelligent people after him, have persuaded him and his followers to come back.

So you must easily see, how difficult a task it is, to keep so capricious a sett. of people anyways steady.

I have applied to this Province for their Aid and Assistance in furnishing me with Interpreters, Conductors, and such a proportion of presents for the Indians, as they should judge wou'd fall to their Share, considering that So. Carolina and Virginia had both contributed largely, but the Governor has been told by the provinciall Commissioners, that they had no Money, and consequently could allow nothing for that so necessary Service. So that I foresee the whole Expence of the Indians will (in spite of what I can do) fall upon the Crown. I should therefore be extreamly Happy to find what I have hitherto done approved of by His Majesty with Orders how I am to proceed and conduct myself for the future.

As the Artillery, Arms, Tents &ca. destined for the Service in the Southern Provinces are not yet arrived, nor any Accounts of them, I have been obliged to scrape together some Guns of different Calibres

from different places, with all the Ammunition—and three Royal Howbitzers that I have got cast here, in order to form a train, which, with
the Assistance of an Officer and nine Men of our own train, that General Abercromby has been so good as to send me, and what I can pick
out from among the Provincialls, I hope in some Measure to be able
to supply the Disappointment of the Store Ship, and Artillery Men.
Having bought and borrowed a good many Firelocks, and provided 300
Tents, which in warm weather must serve them all, as every Man has
a Blankett. I have now on the back Frontiers of this Province three
Months Provisions for 6000 Men, and I am just entering into a contract for a sufficient number of Waggons and Pack-horses for the
transportation of it from one deposite to another, as soon as the
troops can be brought up and pushed forward to prepare those stockaded deposites for the reception of the provisions and stores.

I shall lose no time in getting everything in readyness to move
forward, as by that Means I may facilitate General Abercromby's
operation, by preventing the West Country Indians from going to join
the Canadians upon Lake George.

As I have severall people out for Intelligence I hope in a short
time to inform you of the Enemy's Strength, and my Generall plan
for annoying the Enemy, and shall by the first opportunity, send you
a Draught of the Country, with the march I intend to make.

I am Sr. with the greatest respect & regard

Yr. most obt. & most humle. Servt.

Jo: Forbes.

To Governor Sharpe
Archives of Maryland, v.9, p.188

Sir.

I Have the favour of Yours of the 14th which I should have Ac-
knowledged, had it come sooner to my hands.

I must Confess that your Assemblys breaking up without Con-
curring in any way with His Majesty's Demands, is such a Piece of
Presumption that Deserves a much Severer Chastisement, than I shall
pretend to think of.

Your Goodness, Sir, in Attaching yourself to a few of your Militia, to go upon the Frontiers, shows well your good Inclinations to
Serve the Publick in those most trying times.

I am greatly at a loss, & much Distressed how to Act with regard to the 300 Men, that you had at Fort Cumberland and Frederick
in the Province pay. As you have said Nothing about them, I hope
they continue as they were, untill I have the pleasure of seeing you.
At the same time, should be well pleased that they could be all got
together at Fort Cumberland as by that means part of Colonel Washington's Virginia Regt might march to Fort Frederick, in order to

Joyn the other Troops at Rays Town, but as you will see Sir John St Clair, I think those things may be easily Settled for the best.

I am Extremely obliged to Capt Dagworthy & the officers at Fort Cumberland, and I am very Sorry that their good Endeavors to gett Intelligence, has not mett with the Desired Success.

Our Friends the Indians in those parts & the Cherokees ought to have Signals to know Each other by to prevent Mischieff.

Neither our Artillery, nor the Highland Regt are yet Arrived, so I cannot say when I can leave this, but am always, with real regard,

Sir

Yr most Obt & most

Humble Servt

Philadelphia May 25th 1758   Jo. fforbes

To William Pitt

Correspondence of William Pitt with colonial governors in America, v.1, p.278

Philadelphia. June 17th.. 1758.

Sir,

Colo. Montgomery's Highland Battalion arrived here the Eight from So. Carolina, and I dispatch'd Capt. Mc.Intosh the next day to Admiral Boscawen. The Store Ship with Arms, Tents, Ammunition, & Artillery &ca. arrived here the 11th., which enables me to set out directly for the frontiers, where I have previously assembled all the new Levys of this Province and Virginia. North Carolina I am told has sent 200 Men by sea to Alexandria in Virginia, and have ordered 100 more (which is all they have) to march by the back parts of Virginia in order to join me, at Fort Cumberland, but when they will arrive I cannot tell.

The Maryland Assembly broke up without providing any one thing for the present Service, or for the payt. & maintenance of their troops in Fort Cumberland and Fort Frederick, since the eight of October last. By which the Crown becomes bound by the Earl of Loudoun's orders to Mr. Sharpe, for the payment of those Garrisons from October last to the present time, & the necessity of keeping them there, was the preservation of those two Forts from the Enemy. As they are only 300 Men, and have been used to the Woods and the Indian Manner of fighting, I thought it would be a great loss to allow them to disband themselves, upon the province refusing them their by past pay, or continuing them during the Campaign; so have therefore made them an offer to pay them from this time during the rest of the Campaign, and to solicite for their by past pay, either from the Province, or by Virtue of the Earl of Loudoun's promise and orders to Governour Sharpe.

The Cherokee Indians are, (I am afraid) no longer to be kept with us, owing to their natural fickle disposition which is not to be got the better off by fair words nor presents, of both which they have had a great deal, and threats we dare not use, least they change sides, so if the seeing of our Cannon and their Cousins the Highlanders has no Effect upon their stay with us, we shall lose the best part of our Strength as all the Northern Indians mostly our Enemies were kept in awe by the presence of so many Cherokees. As my offensive Operations are clogged with many Difficultys, owing to the great distance & badness of the roads, through an almost impenetrable wood, uninhabited for more than 200 Miles, our back inhabitants being all drove into Carlisle. I am therefore lay'd under the Necessity of having a stockaded Camp, with a Blockhouse & cover for our Provisions, at every forty Miles distance. By which Means, altho' I advance but gradually, yet I shall go more Surely by lessening the Number, and immoderate long train of provision Waggons &c, For I can set out with a fortnight's provisions from my first deposite, in order to make my second, which being finished in a few days, and another fortnight's provision, brought up from the first, to the second, I directly advance to make my third, and so proceed forward, by which I shall have a constant Supply security for my provisions, by moving them forward from Deposite, to Deposite as I advance, and lastly if not thought convenient to settle upon the Ohio, or in that Country, I shall have a sure retreat, leaving a road always practicable to penetrate into those back Countrys, as our Settlements advance towards them, from this side of the Allegany Mountains.

I need not point out to you, Sir, my reasons for these precautions, when you consider that had our last Attempt upon Fort Du Quesne succeeded, we must have retired directly, for want of provisions, and at that time our back Settlements were much nearer advanced to Fort Du Quesne and the Ohio, than they are at present, having properly speaking none to the Westward of Carlisle.

I have used every art and Means to get Intelligence of the strength of the French and Indians (in their Alliance) in those parts, but to little purpose, having various reports, which may indeed be true, as their Savages may be as whimsical as ours, and consequently they may have sometimes numbers and at other times few or none. But by every Account the whole of them in those parts are in a starving Condition, as there has no Provisions been sent to them this Year, either from Canada, nor by the Missippi. . . . As the Store Ship was so late of Coming in, I was obliged to purchase a great many Arms, Tents &c, for the Provincialls, so shall keep the supernumerary Arms in Store, and the new Tents may serve another occasion—I have likewise been obliged to purchase every kind of thing for the Indians who came naked, having had no manner of Assistance from either off the Superintendants of Indian Affairs.

I have now above 400 Men out upon scouting partys, but as they have four or five Hundred miles in the going and returning, what Intelligence they bring is always of so old a date that there is no trusting to it.

I shall lose no Time in doing every thing in my power for the publick good to the best of my Capacity, and have the honour to be, with the greatest regard and esteem. Sir, Y^r. most obed^t. & most humble Servt.

Jo: Forbes.

To Governor Sharpe
Archives of Maryland, v.9, p.209

Philad: Iune 20th [1758]

Sir,

I Give you the trouble of this very short Letter, to Acknowledge your Favors, and the Sense I have of your Zeal for His Majesty's Service.

The Enclosed Letter from Mr Kilby, our Contractor for provisions, will show you I have taken the first opportunity of making Dr Ross easy as to what he has furnished, and I hope very soon to Enable you to make those Officers & Troops that were at F. Cumberland Easy as to the past, and I do myself Engage for the present pay, while they remain in the King's Service, during this Campaign.

I shall order Tents, Canteens &c. for them, and send them up as soon as possible.

Colonel Bouquet & Sir John St Clair Writes me of the Road you propose from Fort Frederick to Cumberland; If it is thought the most Eligible, you will be very obliging in giving a look to it, and your Directions to those Employed to make it. Any Advances of money for the present to Clear the by past pay or Expence of the Maryland Troops, must by no means diminish, or Interfere with our Claim for the same from the Province.

I have been much out of Order, but am much

Y^r most Ob^t & most
Hum^{ble} Servt
Jo: fforbes

To Governor Sharpe
Archives of Maryland, v.9, p.219

Head Quarters at Carlisle July the 8th 1758.

Sir

I have received from General Abercromby an Extract of a Letter to the Governour General of Canada, in relation to the Capitulation of

Fort William Henry; which Extract I send your Honour inclosed with General Abercrombys order in consequence of it.

I am with great Regard

Your Honours

Most obedient Humble Servt

Jo: fforbes

To the Reverend Mr. Barton

Pennsylvania Archives, ser. 1, v.3, p.451

Sir,

I am sorry to find that the Troops of the Communion of the Church of England, are not properly provided with a Clergyman of their own Profession.

In consequence therefore, of your laudable zeal for the Service of your King & Country, & of your truly commendable inclination of discharging your ministerial and Episcopal duty to the Troops under my command,

You are hereby invited & authorized to the Discharge of all Ministerial functions belonging to a Clergyman of the Church of England, amongst the Troops under my Command. And all & sundry, are hereby order'd and requir'd, to pay all due Reverence & Respect to you & the Reverend functions you are invested with. And be assured, Sir, that in all places & at all times, the Clergymen, & those of the Church of England, shall always be properly encouraged & protected.

I am, Revd Sir,

Your most obedient &

Most humble Serv't,

Jo. Forbes.

Carlisle, July 9th, 1758.

To William Pitt

Correspondence of William Pitt with colonial governors in America, v.1, p.294

Carlisle Camp west of Susquehannah. July 10th. 1758.

Sir

I did myself the honour of writing to you from Philadelphia the 17th of June, when I acquainted you of the Situation of the Troops under my Command. So soon as I gott the Artillery and Stores landed from on board the transports from England, and putt in some Order which was not till the 30th. of June, I sett out from Philadelphia with the Highland Battalⁿ. of Montgomery and the train of Artillery which marches into the Camp here this day, all well and in order, altho the March was long being 120 miles in excessive hot weather, and having two great Rivers the Skulkill and Susquehannah to pass, upon Rafts and Flatts, and the last river being 1900 yards over. I halt tomorrow and shall then proceed 100 miles further to Raestown, where I have now 1500 of the Provincialls, who are building some Storehouses and stockading a piece of Ground for our Ammunition and provisions. For in Raestown there is not one single house; The place having its name from one Rae, who designed to have made a plantation there several years ago, nor indeed is there either Inhabitants or houses from this to the Ohio (except at Forts Loudoun and Lyttelton which are only two or three houses each, inclosed with a Stockade of 100 feet square) the whole being an immense Forest of 240 miles of Extent, intersected by several ranges of Mountains, impenetrable almost to any thing humane save the Indians, (if they be allowed the Appellation) who have foot paths, or tracts through those desarts, by the help of which, we make our roads.

I am in hopes of finding a better way over the Alleganey Mountain, than that from Fort Cumberland which Gen^ll. Braddock took, If so I shall shorten both my March, and my labour of cutting the road about 40 miles, which is a great consideration. For were I to pursue M^r. Braddock's route, I should save but little labour, as that road is now a brushwood, by the sprouts from the old stumps, which must be cut down and made proper for Carriages, as well as any other Passage that we must attempt.

The Cherokee Indians being but bad Judges of time, came too early in the year to our Assistance, and therefore had not patience to wait our time, so that from the fickleness of their temper the greatest part of them—went home three weeks ago. You may believe Sir, that no method was left untryed to detain them, but they are like Sheep. where one leaps, all the rest follow.

We have still near 200 that remain, and are so much attached to us that they have given the little nothing they have into our Stores as a pledge of their Services to us during the Campaign.

This is owing in a great degree to M^r. Byrd of Virginia to whom I should do a great injustice if I was silent upon the Occasion.—As he has a very large and opulent fortune in Virginia he joined the Earl of Loudoun early after his Arrival in America, Accompany'd the Army to Halifax last year, and sett a noble example to all the Gentlemen of the Continent, who had either Inclination or Abilities to serve the King and their Country.

He in the Month of February last offered his Services to the Earl of Loudoun, and embarked at New York for South Carolina, went from thence some hundreds of Miles up into the Cherokees Country, assembled their Chiefs, and by a march of near a thousand Miles conducted some of the best warriors of that Nation through both the Carolina and Virginia into this Country, and luckily arrived in time at the Army (then in Embryo) where by his Interest and the sight of His followers, their Countrymen, and Chief Sachems; The number I now have the honor to acquaint you off, remains steady to His Majesty's Service, and are now the advanced Guard of the troops under my Command: The Virginia Assembly have named him to the Command of their new raised regim^t, which he accepted off with pleasure, and actuated by the same spirit and Zeal for the Honour of the King and good of his Country, has I dare say at great personall expence equipt his regim^t in many necessaries not allowed of by the Virginia Assembly, and they are now all ready at Fort Cumberland.

You will pardon me Sir if I mention one other Gentleman, who tho a near relation of mine, I cannot but do his Intentions and Endeavours the Justice they deserve, I mean M^r. Glen, late Governour of S^o. Carolina, who came from thence with Montgomery's regim^t. to pay me a visit at Philadelphia, where hearing of the Defection and falling off, of the Cherokees, went off into the back Countrys directly, and as he has had formerly great dealings with them, I am persuaded his personall Interest among them, contributed greatly at this present time in making them do whatever is desired. But I am persuaded that a Message that he has sent to the little Carpenter, who is the second person of the whole Cherokee Nation will bring him and some of his Warriors to join us before the end of the Campaign, so that, as to the point of Indians, we shall be very well if they continue steady, but that is precarious; As the least jealousy, or smallest disgust, oversetts a months Civility, and good usage at once.

In my last, I had the honour to acquaint you, How that the Maryland Assembly had behaved with regard to His Majesty's Orders, communicated to them by you.

So glaring an Infraction of his Majesty's Royal Command at this critical time, draws the eye of all upon them; and their refusing all aid, and assistance, for their own protection, and repelling the Enemy, strikes all honest Men with a horrible Idea of their Ingratitude to the best of Kings.

I am with the greatest regard and esteem

      y^r. most ob^t. & most Hum^{ble}. Servt.

           J^o. Forbes.

To Governor Sharpe

Archives of Maryland, v.9, p.235

Camp at Carlisle Iuly 20th 1758.

Sir

Having considered what you have told me concerning the Situation of Your Maryland Troops, and particularly about the Distressed Condition of the Officers, and of M^r. Ross, by whom your Forces have been Victualled (since the money which was granted by your Assembly for their Support was Expended) and being very Averse to your

Troops being Disbanded at this Critical Juncture, when in all probability I shall have great occasion for their Service, I am induced to Advance a Sum of money towards Relieving those Gentlemen in some measure from the Difficulties, wherein they are Involved by the late Extraordinary Conduct of Your Assembly, & to Encourage your Troops to keep together during the Campaign.

As I do not take upon myself to pay your Troops the Arrears that are due to them, or to Satisfy Mr Ross, but Expect that your Assembly will, out of the Supplies which they shall grant at their next meeting, Appropriate a Sum for those purposes, I shall not Concern myself with any Accounts whatever; that I leave to your Assembly, or to such persons as you or they may Appoint, but what I Advance, I Advance upon the Credit of the Province, to be Repaid me out of the first money that your Assembly may Raise, & I Desire you will Communiate this Letter to them, that they may be thoroughly Apprised of my Intentions & Expectations.

As I Doubt not but your Assembly will notwithstanding what has lately happened be Satisfied with my keeping Your Troops together till the End of the Campaign, I shall not Scruple to Assure them that they will most certainly be paid as long as they shall Continue in the Service.

I am, with great Regard, &c   Y^r Excellencies

Most Ob^t and

most Hum^{ble} Servt

Jo: fforbes.

To Governor Sharpe
Archives of Maryland, v.9, p.238

Dear Sir

I can not paint the misery and distress that I have been in since I had the pleasure of seeing you, by that damnd Flux, which I hope has now made its last effort by knocking me up some days ago at this blessed habitation, I now begin to mend a little, and hope in a day or two to gitt forward, where tho my presence be necessary, yet my absence creates no stop in carrying on our publick affairs, our new road advancing apace, so that in a few days I hope to have our advanced post on the other side of Laurell Hill pretty well advanced towards the Enemy.

My Gripes obliges me to make use of another Hand writing than my own which I know you have goodness enough to excuse as likewise the freedom that Major Halkett used with you two days ago in desiring you would order some of your Correspondents to Buy 2 or 300 pair of Blanketts and send them directly to Raestown, by the first and readiest opportunity that can be procured.

I send you the enclos'd packett and beg the favour that you will further it by Express to Williamsburg, as I really neither know the best nor nearest way of sending it, so shall leave Apolligizing any further till I have the pleasure of seeing you. Quere if I should march strait out, could you take the Garrison of Fort Cumberland under the protection of your Militia for a fortnight or so, in order that I might strengthen myself with all the Virginians that I shall other ways be obliged to leave there.

There is a talk this morning but with what foundation I know not as if Louisbourg should have been surrendered the 22^d of last month but this surely cannot be true altho we are in daily expectations of good news from that quarter.

I am with real sincerity   My Dear Sir

             Y^r most obed^t &

               most hum^{ble} Servt

Shippensburg 16th August   Jo: fforbes

To Governor Sharpe
Archives of Maryland, v.9, p.240

Shippensburg 23^d August 1758.

Dear Sir

The Enclosed Letters have given me great uneasiness, as I am sure they will do the same to you; It is Indeed greatly owing to a mistake of my own, or rather my Sickness, that prevented my Writing fully upon this Head to Mr Kilby or Mr Howell, and sending Credit for the Moneys Drawn above the 1500 £ Sterling that Mr Kilby had ordered payment for; and I really Imagined that I had not presumed upon his paying any more, except the Difference betwixt the 600 £ Sterling, & the 850 £, which I Imagined would meet no Stop, having Desired Major Halkett to write so to M^r McAdam, his Son in Law, and which I could have Replaced at any time. I fancy you understood it in this Light likewise, & that the Sum Exceeding this 1750 Sterling, was rather an Advance for me, than money that I required Mr Kilby to pay, who no doubt in this Affair Behaved with great Spirit, having Advanced the 1500 £ in the frankest manner, & taking the Chances of Payment, as he Writes in his Letter.

The other Summs I certainly ought to have given Warrants for (but then, as at present Confounded by Distemper, I had not Sense to Reflect upon, or Write about them) so We must now Sett it to rights as soon as possible, to Relieve Dr Ross of his punctilio, in which I do not see so much hurt, as perhaps he does, nor do I think it would have been very much blamed, had he Restored Mr Howell the Money for the Bills, untill the Affair had been Cleared up; because by that means he would have prevented the Imprisonment & have given me the time to have made all Easy.

The Case as it appeared to me, and still does, is thus—That as a Large Sum of Money was due to the Maryland Troops, for different Articles, from October last, to, I shall suppose May, Mr Kilby, upon the Acco^{tt} of the Articles concerning Provisions &c. agreed to the Advance of 1500 £ Sterling on Account; to promote the Service & to prevent a totall Stop; knowing that my hands & Inclinations were both tied up by General Abercromby's not thinking himself sufficiently Authorized to fulfill Ld Loudoun & Genl Stanwix's orders. That upon this Advance of Mr Kilby's, I should likewise give so much more Money to account, in order to Enable the people, who had been Employed, to keep their Credit, & to proceed in furnishing the Troops as formerly.

That therefore those Summs to be thus Advanced were upon the General Accompt, & not Destined to the payment of any particular Demand, as the Accotts with their Vouchers had not been properly looked over & Liquidate; and as by this means we had our Claims upon the Province for such Summs advanced for the Use of their Troops, & that to be backed by you, & the people who had furnished & Supported the Troops, particularly as they would have upon the Whole greater Summs due to them than we were to Advance.

In Consequence of this, the Bills Drawn upon Mr Howell, or Mr Kilby, has allarmed him, as perhaps he Imagined that I was to turn the whole over upon him, when in reality I Understood I was only making him pay 1750 £ Sterling in place of 1500; and that I was to Advance the rest of the money for the payment of those Bills, upon the General without Specifying the time, or the purpose for what the Money was Advanced, so fancy I have no other way but to send a Warrant upon Mr Neilson of Philadelphia for the summ agreed to be paid, that Exceeds the £1500 pound, to be paid by Mr Kilby. But I do not well understand Mr Ross's Letter to you, wherein he says, on the 15th Mr Howell paid him £510 Curr^y the Bill of Exchange of £2976. 15. Curr^y & the order of £850 Sterling, in all 2770. 9. 8, in full of two last orders, and a little after says, that Mr Howell Insisted on his Returning him Bills for £1270. 9. 8 & the 510£ Curr^y All this I cannot unravel, or know how these Summs come either to be Disjoined, or linked together. As I thought the Whole money to be Advanced was a Generall one not Adequate, or appropriate to the Defraying of any particular Charge, & of which Kilby was to give Creditt for so much, and I so much more.

By the Return of the Express you will be so good as Explain this to me, & point me out the Way, how that Dr Ross is to be Relieved, which I shall most readily Comply with, but be so good as to Remember that the money paid by Sir John St Clair, must be looked upon as so much money paid by me, & what I must Charge myself with.

I Thank you for yours of the 21st and I am very much Obliged to you, for your offer of taking care of F^t Cumberland which will be a

great help to me; but I do not think that I shall want your People
before the Week after next, altho' my new Road is quite ready the
length of Laurelbridge, & I have sent to take post on the other Side of
it, from whence it is all good to the Ohio. But I Expect a great meeting of the Indians, when they must Determine Friends or Foes: I
Fancy they'll Choose the Last, as they are now Scalping within a mile
of this, and I have only 50 men with me, but I Expect 200 Highlanders
this Night, so if possible shall Endeavor to way lay them, but this does
not look as if they were Courting a Peace.

I am obliged to you for your Care of the Blankets, and shall send
you from this an order for the money payable at Annapolis, if agreeable to you there.

I Have been very bad, but better since Yesterday, & shall sett out
for Raes Town when able to bear Travelling.

I am

Dr Sir.   Yr most Obt
                                     most humble Servt
                                     Jo: fforbes

I shall Write to you soon when your people will be wanted at Cumberland

I must beg you will send me a Copy of the Enclosed Letters.

To David Ross
Pennsylvania Magazine, v.33, p.86

Shippensburg 28th August 1758

Sir

I designd to have wrote you the other day when I sent Mr. Howell
credit for the money paid into your hands over and above the £1500
Sterling allowed to be paid by Mr. Kilby, but I was so much out of
order that I was not able.

I am sorry that this transaction designed almost entirely for your
behoof, and the carring on of the service, should have turned out so
disagreeably, nor could I have imagined that you was to conceive
either Governour Sharp's honour or your own so deeply concerned as
to choose to go to Prison rather than return Mr. Howell that money,
when a little reflection must have suggested to you that some misun-
derstanding or neglect had been the cause of Mr. Howell's redemand-
ing it, which a letter to me must have cleared up imediately.

As the neglect was mine I hope you have now got the money, I
am therefore now to acquaint you in order to prevent misunderstand-
ings betwixt Governour Sharp and me that you are not to pay away
that whole sum untill that you hear farther from Governr Sharp, as
this money advanced by me is designed as a Generall aid to diminish
the debts due by and to, the Maryland troops, and for the carrying

Pittsburgh in 1790, from the original sketch by Lewis Brantz

on of the service, and not at all designed to the paying of any particular debt due in this manner, I mean transporting provisions, officers or mens pay, hospitals &c^a because, before those can be fully cleared the Accounts and the Vouchers must be properly examined and found relavant.

So therefore I would not have you use above £500 of the above sum untill that you hear farther from me or the Governour, and that only to stop the mouths of poor people who may be in want, the rest of the sum remaing in your hands accountable for it to me.

I hope to see the Governour in a few days when all this will be easily adjusted I am Sir

Your most obed^t

Most humb^{le} Servt

Jo.Fforbes

To Richard Peters

Pennsylvania Magazine, v.33, p.87

Sir   Shippensburg 28 August (1758).

I wrote you by Mr Ennis the Express two days ago, and have little to add, only my distemper begins to abate.

I know that your Coffee house people will make their remarks very freely why I do not proceed but they must talk; altho' I must take my own way. But the great reason is, the horrible roguery, and rascality in the Country people, who did not at all fulfill their Contracts and agreements, neither in Carriages nor Horses. For in the place of Carrying 2000 w^t they never had above 14 or 1500, and in place of 12 days made 20 of their Journeys by which our magzines were dissapointed and our daily consumption at Raestown must have fallen upon them (the Magazines) had I pushed forward the troops.

Everything that depended upon the troops has succeeded to admiration, and we have got intirely the better of that impossible road, over the Alleganey mountain & Laurell ridge, so we are ready to take the very first favourable opportunity (if not with the whole) at least of visiting the Enemy with pretty large detachments. So that now my advancing will again depend upon the honesty of the Inhabitants by their furnishing proper or improper Carriages, and which I beg you will make known to every body, as the troops are in great spirits, but I must not lead them to fall a sacrafice to want or Famine, and the price I pay and the treatment the Waggoners and horses meet with, deserves a better return from the Inhabitants, than they have as yet shown, for which their Country may suffer severely in the End.

I hope we have chaced off the Enemy Indians from this neighbourhood, having had 300 Highlanders with all the best woodsmen out these 3 days, night and day, but never could have the Good fortune of falling on with any of them.

Two of the Indians fired upon the Head of a party of ours of 80 men, yet notwithstanding they were Instantaneously pursued they gott away. The whole Country has been in a pannick but begin again to revive. They are a sett of helpless heartless mortalls.

Col⁰ Byrd writes me from Fort Cumberland that a large party of Enemy Indians have been in that neighbourhood, and that Capt Bullen and Capt French who had just brought 50 Catawbas to our assistance, coming from Winchester, would go before the party when they come near Fort Cumberland, by which means they were attacked by 9 Indians, killed, and scalped within a mile of the Fort. This is a very great loss, as Bullen had proved himself a sincere friend to us.

A party of ours have returned from the Ohio with two scalps which I shall endeavour to get you, they were within a half mile of Fort Duquesne, but do not say anything extraordinary, only thinks there were about 50 Tents near the Fort and reckons there may be as many Indians there as tents, and a Garrison of 3 or 400 men.

But as this is all Conjecture, and that hitherto in spite of all the partys I have sent out, I can learn nothing that is to be depended upon, I must therefore beg that Andrew Montour may be forthwith employed in getting me Intelligence of the Enemys Strength in those parts, by going himself, as likewise sending 2 or 3 trusty hands to pick up what they can learn, as to the number of the French Canadians or Indians there at present, or expected, wether they have thrown up any Entrenchments before the Fort betwixt the Ohio and Mononga-hela. What they have built lately either at the Fort or tother side of the river. What Guns they mount in the Fort, wether they send out partys from the Fort during the day or night to reconnoitre the Environs. How many men mount Guard daily, &c &c and the dis-position of the Indians. These spies may return to our advanced post 9 miles forward from Loyall Hannon on the other side of the Chestnut ridge of Mountains and about 40 miles from Fort Du Quesne. They may make themselves known by wearing yellow Fillets about their heads and Arms, and waving of their matchcoats upon a long pole.

I am in want of spying Glasses to send out with my partys so pray buy for me two or three good ones, and send up by the very first Express. Let Mr. Croghan send out people likewise with the same directions, and I shall be very glad to see him after your Congress, which I hope still goes forward and will produce something. I should be glad to know if they were Delawares, that was here the other day. I dare say everything will be said to bring the Indians to see their own Interest, and to abandon the French, and I fancy any demands that they have to make will be so moderate, as to be asily complyed with, and doubt not but many of their young men may be induced to join me, In which case Mr. Croghan would do a signall service in conducting them safe to me. Let Mr. West purchase 50 llb. weight of Vermillion, and send it off, with the first waggons that come up from Mr. Howell, with proper directions. I have broke my little Barometer, I wish you could purchase me another and send it me up safe.

Hambies & Teedyuscungs son goes down to Easttown to persuade their friends to come and join me, I wish they may be sincere so pray let them be watched narrowly.

I hope the Province will make no difficulty, as to the Expence of this meeting, as it will be a most monsterous reflection upon them if they do, and they never after can either look for, or expect the favour or protection of Great Brittain.

I stand greatly in need of a few prunes by way of Laxative, if any fresh are lately arrived a few pounds will be a great blessing, or a pound 2 or 3 of such fine raisins as Mr. Allen's were, as I eat nothing.

I expect all the news of Louisburgh so dont baulk me—

I am Dr Sir most sincerely yrs &c &c
Jo Fforbes

General Forbes' Instructions to Major Shippen
Pennsylvania Magazine, v.33, p.90

Major Shippen. You are to order the 2 new Levyed Companys of ———— to march without loss of time to strengthen the Garrison of Fort Augusta leaving one Officer and 30 men at Fort Hunter.

All the rest of the new levyed Companys are to march towards Lancaster and so up to Carlisle, where they will have tents provided for them.

The Arms and camp necessarys for those Companys levyed up the Country, ought to be sent to Lancaster or Carlisle, as those towns lyes most contiguous to the Companys. You are to wait upon Sr John St Clair if he is at Carlisle, who will give you his orders about the marching up of these companys to the Camp at Carlisle, From whence a Detatchment equall to the Garrisons of the Forts may be made from the whole, and the companys now there may be brought on to join the army.

To Governor Sharpe
Archives of Maryland, v.9, p.261

Shippensbourg 3^d September 1758

Sir

By a letter from Mr Howell at Philadelphia dated August 30th I find Dr Ross's affair not fully settled, altho by the return of your Express I sent Mr Howell credit for £1519..18..8 Sterling to reimburse him for the money advanced to Dr Ross over and above £1500 sterling allowed off by Mr Kilby; This as far as I could account was the whole sum; but Mr Howell writes me that Dr Ross received from him £2770..9..8 Sterling in Bills of Exchange, besides £510 Currency, which two sums is some hundreds more than the £3019..18..8.. sterling paid By Mr Kilby and me, but Mr Howell says that Mr Kilby is to be there in a day or two, who will easily set those matters to rights; So there is the less matter as Mr Ross is not, nor never was in prison, and might have prevented all this trouble by returning Mr Howell the Bills he had had from him, which I find he must do at last, as Mr Howell writes me that he believes I must send new Bills at last to prevent some losses, or some other things which I understand nothing off, such as Course of Exchange &c.

I must take notice of Dr Ross's indiscretion who when Mr Howell proposed to him to lodge the Bills and Cash in any indifferent persons Hands untill Mr Kilby or I could send our instructions about the affair, refused positively to do so, giving as his reason that as he had now got hold, he would not let go, which answer obliged Mr Howell to take the steps he did, and must of consequence oblige Mr Kilby and me to take proper receipts from Dr Ross for the money we advance upon the General account as neither his acc^{ts} nor Vouchers have been looked over by us, or properly authenticated, for us to advance money upon, you will therefore be so good as write the D^r upon this subject and acquaint him that whatever money he receives now, he must be accountable for, and therefore ought to make no payments nor reimbursements without your particular allowance, as you know some of the accounts may upon examination admit of disputes unless very clearly Vouched.

I must likewise add that the sum I have ordered payment for to Dr Ross greatly exceeds what Mr Kilby and I at first thought necessary to be advanced, for supporting the Drs Credit and further carrying on the service, so it, will be necessary before you allow the D^r to pay away that money advanced by me, that I have a Copy of the D^{rs} accounts sent me, and that those articles not clearly vouched be the last that any money is paid upon.

I propose leaving this to morrow morning in a kind of Horse litter, being so weakened by my distemper that I neither can ride nor bear the roughness of my slopwaggon However I hope a few days will make a great change.

I have wrote to Col^o Bouquet of your kind agreement of Garrisoning Fort Cumberland for the first month of my absence, and that 250 of your men would be there by the 10th or 12th Instant, ordering the Commissary to furnish them with provisions and a Gill of spirits each p day during their stay in that service, If there be any thing more wanted let me know, or if when there, you find any other thing necessary you will be so good as to order it, as the Commissary shall have directions to do whatever you require. Pray let me know if you have heard of the Blanketts.

I give you joy of Louisbourg which is certainly a great Acquisition and may be of some service to me, for as I dont hear that they have reinforced Fort Du Quesne with any Regulars, I fancy their chief reliance may be upon the Western Indians from Detroit, who as Mr Croghan writes me will certainly leave them soon; this with the numbers of Delaware nations and other tribes going now to treat with us at East town prevents my hurrying measures for some days, least by a precipitate blow I might prevent the success of the treaty at East town; and the only thing I dread the French will do, is they will persuade the West country Indians in Conjunction with the shawenese to come and attack the head of my Army now taking post on the other side Laurell hill, before that the Indians return home, what are your sentiments thereupon? wether to proceed with the whole, or temporize a few days longer, untill that we see how the East town treaty turns out, where I wish heartily you could have been, as you must know any Indian friendship at this critical time might prove a great dimunition to the strength of the French.

I foresee I shall be in great distress for want of waggons, the Horses of those with me being ruined as they say for want of forage, a neglect that Sir John St Clair can never answer for, who was sent from Philadelphia by me to make magazines of Forage all along the march route and to have a great Quantity in store at Raestown,

I am D^r S^{ir}
Y^r most obed^t &
most hum^{le} Servt
Jo: fforbes

To William Pitt

Correspondence of William Pitt with colonial governors in America, v.1, p.338

Fort Loudoun. the 6th. September. 1758.

Sir

In my last letter I had the honour to acquaint you, of my proceedings in the new road across the Alleganey Mountains, and over Laurell Hill, (leaving the Rivers Yohiegany and Monongahola to my left hand) strait to the Ohio, by which I have saved a great deal of way, and prevented the misfortunes that the overflowing of those rivers might occasion I acquainted you likewise of the suspicions I had of the small trust I could repose in the Pennsylvanians in assisting of me with any one necessary, or any help in furthering the Service that they did not think themselves compelled to do by the words of your letter to them.

As likewise of almost the total defection and desertion of the Southern Indians (except 80) who after the receiving of their presents &c, have all returned home not without committing egregious outrages upon the scattered Inhabitants of the Northwest parts of Virginia in their return.

I thought fit to recapitulate this least my letters dont come to hand regularly as there is no post in those parts, nor any regular one anywhere except from Philadelphia, By New York, to Boston; and even there one may be three Months in receiving a Letter, that ought to be delivered in ten days, besides my letters must now go by Mercht. Ships, which makes the delivery very precarious. I hinted to you in my former, of my endeavouring to bring about a Treaty betwixt the Delaware Indians &ca., neighbours to those Provinces, but of late drove into the Arms of French and removed to the Ohio, as the Indians demands were but few, and to me seeming not unreasonable, I thought the reclaiming of those Tribes would be of very great Service to the Publick in weakening of the French Interest by seting a good example to other Western Tribes of Indians, who it is said have all the Inclination to be well with us, wanting only an Opportunity, and an Assurance of protection to declare themselves for us, or at least to remain neutralls.

This is almost brought to a Crisis, their Chief Men being hourly expected at East-town upon the Delaware, where the Governr. of Pennsylvania and Jersey are to meet them and settle Preliminaries; I wish it could have been done sooner, and that they could have had time to remove, because now my scene of offensive Operations must imediately be put in Execution, when it will be hard for me to distinguish betwixt our friendly disposed Indians, and our real Enemies.

My advanced post consisting of 1500 Men, are now in possession of a strong post 9 Miles on the other side of Laurell Hill, and about 40 from Fort Du Quesne, nor had the Enemy ever suspected my attempting such a road till very lately, they having been all along securing the strong passes, and fords of the rivers, upon General Braddock's route.

My greatest distress and what may be a real hindrance to me for some days is the provisions, which altho' every care imaginable has been taken by contracting for great Numbers of Waggons and Baggage horses at very great Expence. Yet all has not been able, to supply the present consumption, and the maintaining of three Month's Provisions in store to carry along with us—This I early foresaw and acquainted the Governr:, and the Assembly Commissioners of my Doubts, arising from the villiany of the Inhabitants in furnishing their worst Horses at so critical a juncture,—By contract they being obliged to carry 2000lb. wt. p Waggon, such a length of road in such a specified time, but cannot carry above 1400 at most and take up four and twenty days in place of twelve to execute it in.

I have wrote the Governr. in very strong Terms upon this head, beging he would shew it to their Assembly now sitting, in order that they may fall upon Methods of sending from Philadelphia, and parts adjacent, three Months provisions at once, they having Carriages in abundance, and I promising to pay so much p. hun^d.. w^t. for everything delivered into our Generall store at Raestown Camp—This I hope is so reasonable that they will comply with it, altho' sad experience makes me dread that their dilatory Measures, and contrary factions, will so retard, so absolutely necessary a transport as to throw me, and the little Army I have the honour to command, into very great distress.

I was greatly afraid that the unfortunate stop Genl^l. Abercrombie met with, might have enabled the French to strengthen themselves with regulars in those parts, but from every Intelligence I can possibly get, any reinforcements that have joined, or are likely to join them, are the West Country Indians, who returned from Ticonderoga, who likewise may tire at Fort Du Quesne, but of this I hope to be better informed, when still a little nigher them, by the Means of deserters of whom as yet we have not had one come in, and there is but little trust to be put in the best Spies you can find, or in the small scouting parties that you send for discovery, & no truth at all to be expected from an Indian.

The Govern^r. of Maryland I am greatly obliged to, having personally acted with the greatest zeal for the Service, first by sending 50 Voluntiers all good Woods Men to join me, and now by marching 200 of his Militia (I believe contrary to his Assembly's inclination) to Garrison Fort Cumberland for one month or to the 12th. of October. As he stands bound for the pay and the keeping together the Maryland Troops at Fort Cumberland from the 8th. of October last, (to the beginning of May, that I retained them in the Service of the Government) by which that Fort and Country was prevented from falling into the Enemy's hands, all which he did by positive Orders from the Earl of Loudoun, and the same repeated in very strong terms by Brig^r. Gen^{ll}. Stanwix to him, and even to the Commanding Officers of Companys.

This has induced me to give him to the Extent of £1500 Sterling, for the present support of his Credit, and the further carrying on of the Service which I hope will meet with your Approbation, as Govern^r. Sharp assures me at the same time, that in his Opinion, the Maryland Assembly now sensible of their by past bad behaviour, will upon their first Meeting pass a law for the payment of all those Accounts.

Govern^r. Dobbs, without previously acquainting me, did send 200 Men by Sea up to join me, and was to send 100 more by land, the first 200 are joined, but the Governour writes me that having neither money nor Credit in their province, he was unable either to furnish them with Cloaths, or send pay along with them, and desires that I would furnish all those and any other Necessaries wanting, and that he would reimburse that expence, out of the first Monies paid by the Crown to that Province, hitherto they have had the King's Provisions, but as they are in want of everything, I must either give them a kind of Cloathing, or get no Service from them.

I vainly at the beginning flattered myself that some very good Service might be drawn from the Virginia, & Pennsylvania Forces, but am sorry to find that a few of their principle Officers excepted, all the rest are an extream bad Collection of broken Innkeepers, Horse Jockeys, & Indian traders, and that the Men under them, are a direct copy of their Officers, nor can it well be otherwise, as they are a gathering from the scum of the worst of people, in every Country, who have wrought themselves up, into a panick at the very name of Indians who at the same time are more infamous cowards, than any other race of mankind.

If it should please God to grant Success to His Majesty's Arms in their Attempts upon the Ohio, and which I think can't well fail, I shall be greatly at a loss how to dispose of Fort Du Quesne, whether to blow it up, and destroy it and the whole Settlements thereabout, or to keep it and leave a Garrison there for the Winter, the execution of the first is as easy, as the second appears to be attended with many difficulties, all which must naturally occur to you, from its great distance from any of the inhabited parts of those Provinces, and consequently the great difficulties of either supporting it, or supplying it with Necessaries during a long severe Winter.

I have consulted the Governours of Pennsylvania and Virginia upon this head, and to know what Number of Troops they could leave there in case it was thought proper to preserve it, to which I have had no positive answer, but I know the Pennsylvania troops will disband the first of December unless their Assembly make a new Provision for their Support.

In a few days I shall have most of my Troops moved forward towards the head, there to be in readyness of seizing the first favourable Opportunity of marching to the Banks of the Ohio, which I now have in my power of doing, by a march of 48 hours, and if refused the Carriages demanded from the Pennsylvanians, or they appear too tardy, and dilatory in the execution thereof, I shall most certainly try it upon flour, and rice, with the Assistance of what live Cattle we can carry forward with us.

My health, that has been extreamly precarious these two years, has of late been very near brought to a close, by a long and severe attack of a bloody flux, which has reduced me to a state of weakness that I am obliged to travel in a Hurdle carried betwixt two Horses but I hope the animating spirits of being able to do the smallest Service to my King and Country, will leave nothing undone on my part that can anyways contribute to the Success of so glorious a cause. I have the honour to be, with the highest esteem and regard, Sir

Y^r. most obed^t. & most hum^{ble}. Servt.

Jo: Forbes

To Governor Denny

Pennsylvania Colonial records, v.8, p.167

Fort Loudoun, Septem^r., 9th, 1758.

Sir:

I have the Honour of laying before you the Situation of His Majesty's Affairs under my Directions in these Southern Provinces at this Critical Juncture, and at the same time to shew you how much it depends on you and the People of this Province to assist in carrying on a Service which his Majesty has so much at Heart, or by their Neglect and Obstinacy have it in their Power to render every step that has been taken (for the safety of these Colonies) fruitless and to no Purpose, but to expend a very great Sum of Money.

The laying in Provisions for the Support of the Army I attempted to do without even being obliged to impress any Carriages. The Quantity of Provisions to have been Collected at our principal Magazine has fallen greatly short of what I had reason to expect, because most of the Waggons were not Loaded with more than Fourteen Hundred Weight, and took a Third more time in the Carriage than they ought to have done, which obliged us to break in upon the Stock of Provisions laid in at Ray's Town, while the Troops were opening a Road over the Mountains, and Securing its Communication, which is now effectually done to within Forty Miles of the French Fort, so that if the Inhabitants who have Waggons are not obliged to furnish a Sufficient Number of them, who, in one Trip to Ray's Town, might Transport the Quantity of Provisions wanted, and where they may receive payment for the Trip at a just and equitable Price, to be fixed by Authority, in Proportion to the Quantity of Provisions so delivered and to the Length of the Journey that they make, the Expedition cannot go forward; nor can I maintain the Ground I am already Master of, but shall be Obliged to draw off my Master's Forces to the Inhabited Parts of the Country, and take Provisions and Carriages wherever they can be found. The Evil which will Attend this Procedure is, that the Innocent must Suffer with the Guilty, and the Exigence of the Case is so pressing as to admit of no delay.

I know there has been several Complaints made of the Scarcity of Forrage, and that several Waggoners has been abused by Officers. If there was any Scarcety of Forrage, it was owing to the Want of Waggons for its Transport; and no Driver ever made his Complaint but the Person who abused him was punished, so that I am induced to believe every Complaint of that kind is without foundation, and, therefore, shall not further insist on a detailed account of the Infamous Breach of Contract on the Part of the Inhabitants.

I have sent to Philadelphia the Quarter Master General, who will explain to you fully the Situation of the Army. I should be sorry to employ him in executing any Violent Measures, which the Exigency of Affairs I am in at present must Compel me to do, if I am not relieved by a Speedy Law for the Providing the Army with Carriages, or a general Concurrence of Magistrates and People of power in those Provinces in assisting, to their utmost, to provide the Same, and that with the greatest Diligence.

Every thing is ready for the Army's Advancing, but that I cannot do unless I have a Sufficient Quantity of Provisions in the Magazines at Ray's Town. The Road that Leads from the advanced Posts to the French Fort may be opėned as fast as a Convoy can march it. Therefore my movement depends on his Majesty's Subjects entering chearfully in carrying up the necessary Provisions. The new Road has been finished without the Enemies knowing it. The Troops having not suffered the least insult in the Cutting it.

And as one Trip of the Waggons will be sufficient for carrying up Provisions to Ray's Town, they shall be paid off at that Place for the Weight they carry and discharged; When they arrive at Ray's Town I shall have nothing to do, but proceed with the Army under my Command, which hitherto have exerted themselves with the greatest Vigor and Spirit, in the great Labour they have undergone; I have done every thing in the Power of Man, to carry on this Expedition with Vigor, if any stop is made to it now, there can be no part laid to my Charge. For this stop you know I have long dreaded, as Six Weeks ago I wrote circular Letters to the Different Magistrates to give all their Aid and Assistance in procuring Waggons to the Contractor's Agents for Transporting Provisions, and that nothing has been neglected that Occur to me for Expediting this so necessary Branch of the Service.

I need not repeat to you the care I have hitherto been at to prevent our Parties from falling upon the Indians, lest, by mistake, it might have fallen upon those who are any wise well disposed to us, and who are, I hope by this time at Easton to meet you, where I hope you will as soon as possible bring things to an Issue, letting the Indians know that the Regard I had for them has been the only reason why I had not long ago fallen upon their Towns, Wives and Children, but that now I could no longer Stop from putting in Execution the Orders of the King, my master, against his Enemies, and all who joined with them.

As you will see Mr. Croghan, you will be so good as to send with those who will follow up to me as soon as possible, and pray, as soon as you can form any idea how matters are likely to turn out, let me know by Express; And I beg your Sentiments as to my Proceedings, if God grant us success against the Enemy; You see the Difficulty of leaving a Garrison there, and you know how your Province have put it out of my power of leaving any of their Troops after the first of December, So I am really at a Loss what step I must take.

I have the honour to be,
Sir, your most obed^t. and Hum^e. Servt.,
John Forbes.

P. S.—As I am willing to embrace every Measure for Carrying on the Service, I have wrote to Several of the Members of the Assembly, to desire their assistance in relation to Carriages, as I suppose you may think it proper to Lay my Letter before them.

Major Grant to General Forbes
Darlington's Fort Pitt and letters from the frontier, p.63

September 14, 1758

Sir:—If it had been in my power to write sooner, you will do me the justice to believe that I should have troubled you long before this time with an account of the detachment which marched the 9th of September from the Camp at Loyal Hanna.

We were lucky enough not to be discovered in our march, though several scouting parties passed very near us. We got to an advantageous post the 12th, about three in the afternoon, which, according to the information of all our guides, was ten or twelve miles from the French fort. I thought it was a proper place to encamp in, as I did not think it advisable to go nearer, for fear of being discovered; but I afterward found that our guides were much mistaken about the distance, for, as near as I can judge, the camp is about sixteen miles from the top of the Hill, where we were to take post. The 13th, at break of day, I sent Major Lewis, with 200 men, and our Indians, with orders to post men in ambuscade, about five miles from the fort, which was all the precaution I could take to prevent our being discovered in the camp. I flattered myself that, if a reconnoitering party was sent out, it might possibly fall into the ambuscade, and, in that case, in all probability they must have been killed or taken; and, if they had sent, in the event our plans succeeding, a second party from the fort, would have found the whole party ready to receive them. I ordered Mr. Chew to march with a party of fifteen or twenty men to reconnoitre the ground and to try, without exposing himself or the men, to draw a party of the enemy into the ambuscade.

He only went with three Indians, who soon left him, and, by that means, in place of returning to Major Lewis' about ten o'clock as I expected, he was obliged to conceal himself till night came on, and he joined me upon the march about eleven o'clock at night. But I would not be understood to reflect upon him; he is a good, brisk young lad. About three in the afternoon I marched forward to the rest of the detachment, and I found Major Lewis advantageously posted about four miles from our camp. The post, I was assured, was not seven miles

from the fort, though I found it was above twelve. After giving
orders to the troops, and particular instructions to the captains, I
proceeded about six in the evening toward the fort, expecting to get
to the top of the Hill about eleven at night; but, as the distance was
so much greater than I imagined, it was after two in the morning before we got there. The instructions, when I left Loyal Hanna, were
that a particular party should be sent to attack each Indian fire,
but, as these fires either had not been made, or were burnt out before
we got to the ground, it was impossible to make any disposition of
that kind. Major Lewis was informed of every particular of our
project before we marched from Loyal Hanna, and was told there
that he was to command the troops that were to be sent upon the
attack. As I was to continue upon the height to make a disposition
for covering his retreat (which we did not desire to be made in good
order) and for forming the rear guard in our march from the fort,
you will easily believe that he and I had frequent conversations upon
the march about our plan of operations. I sent for him the moment
the troops arrived upon the hill opposite the fort, and told him that
as we had been misinformed by the guides in regard to the distance,
and had got there much later than we expected, it was impossible
to make the projected disposition of a party of men for the attack
on each fire; but that it was impossible to continue another day
without being discovered, and that as the night was far advanced,
there was no time to be lost. I therefore ordered him to march
directly, with 100 Americans, 200 Highlanders and 100 Virginians,
and to attack anything that was found about the fort. I gave orders
that no attention should be paid to the sentries, who probably would
challenge, and, in case they were fired upon they were not to return
it upon any account—but to march on as fast as possible—and were
not to fire a shot till they were close to the enemy; and that after
they discharged their pieces they were to use their bayonets without loading a second time. I told the Major that I would order all
our drums and pipes to beat the retreat when it was time for the
troops to relieve, that I was indifferent what order they came back
in, that it was the same thing to me if there was not three of them
together, provided they did the business they were sent upon. The
Major had not half a mile to march into the open plain where the
fort stands, the 400 men under his command had a white shirt over
his clothes to prevent mistakes and that they might even at a distance distinguish one another. I saw the Americans and Highlanders
march off and gave directions that the Virginians should fall in in
the rear. Sending a greater number of men might possibly, I thought,
occasion confusion, and I was of opinion that 400 men were quite
sufficient to carry the service into execution. I was absolutely certain we were not discovered when the troops marched from the hill.
I thought our loss must be inconsiderable, and never doubted but that
everything would succeed beyond our most sanguine expectations.

After posting the remaining part of the troops in the best manner I could, I placed myself and the drums and pipes at the head of the Highlanders who were in the centre and exactly opposite the fort. During the operation the time passed. The day advanced fast upon us, I was turning uneasy at not hearing the attack begin, when to my great astonishment Major Lewis came up and told me "that it was impossible to do any thing, that the night was dark, that the road was bad, worse than anything I had ever seen, that there were logs of wood across it, that there were fences to pass, that the troops had fallen into confusion and that it was a mercy they had not fired upon one another, that they had made so much noise he was sure they must be discovered and that it was impossible for the men to find their way back through those woods." These were really the words he made use of; this behaviour in an officer was new to me; his conduct in overturning a long projected scheme and in disobeying such positive orders was so unaccountable that I could not speak to him with common patience, so that I just made answer to his last words, that the men according to the orders that had been given would have found their way back to the drums when the retreat beat. So I left him and went as fast as I could to Lieutenant McKenzie and Mr. Fisher to see what the matter was and to give directions for the attack if the thing was practicable. I found the troops in the greatest confusion I ever saw men in, which in truth was not surprising, for the Major had brought them back from the plain when he returned himself and everybody then took a road of their own. I found it was impossible to think of forming them for an attack, and the morning was too far advanced to send for the other troops from the other places where they were posted; thus I was reduced, after all my hopes of success, to this melancholy situation. That something at least might be attempted, I sent Lieutenants Robinson and McDonald with fifty men, to make an attack at a place where two or three fires had been seen the night before. I desired them to kill a dozen of Indians if possible, and I would be satisfied. They went directly to the place they were ordered, and finding none of the Indians they set fire to the house, but it was day-light before they could return. I mention this last circumstance that it might appear clearly to you, it was not in my power to send a greater number. The surprise was complete, the governor knew nothing of us or our march, and in all probability the enterprise must have succeeded against the camp as well as against the Indians if the attempt had been made. So favorable an opportunity, I dare say, never was lost.

The difficulties which Major Lewis had represented to me to be insurmountable, appeared to me, as they certainly were, absolutely imaginary. I marched about twelve miles that night, with an advanced guard and flanking parties before it without the least confusion. The Major had not a mile to march to the fort, and above two-thirds of that was in an open plain, and I can safely declare that there is no part of the road in getting into the plain worse than what I had passed without any great difficulty in coming up the hill. I made no secret to the people who were then about me that I was so much dissatisfied with the Major's conduct that I was determined to carry him back to camp in arrest, that he might answer to you for his behaviour. Several officers heard me say so. Mr. Bentinck, if he escaped, has no doubt informed you that such was my intention. However, I did not think it advisable to take any step of that kind till we were out of reach of the enemy. I therefore sent Major Lewis the 14th, at break of day, with the Americans and Virginians to reinforce Captain Bullet, whom I had left with about fifty men as a guard upon our horses and provisions within two miles of the fort, directly upon the road by which we were to return to our camp. I was afraid the enemy might possibly send a detachment that way to take possession of some passes to harass us in our march or perhaps to endeavor to cut us off in case we were forced to make a retreat, and I directed the Major to place these troops in ambuscade that he might have all the advantage possible of any party that could be sent out. About 7 in the morning, after the fog was gone and the day cleared up, it was found impossible to take a plan of the fort from the height where the troops were posted, and as Colonel Bouquet and I had settled that a plan should be taken "a la barke de la Garrise" in case an attempt did not succeed in the night.

I sent Mr. Rhor with Captain McDonald and a hundred men to take the place, with directions not to expose himself or the troops. About the same time, being informed that some of the enemy Indians had discovered Captain McKinzie, who was posted upon the left, almost facing the Monongehela, in order to put on a good countenance and to convince our men they had no reason to be afraid, I gave directions to our drums to beat the Reveille. The troops were in an advantageous post, and I must own I thought we had nothing to fear. In about half an hour after, the enemy came from the fort in different parties without much order, and getting behind trees, they advanced briskly and attacked our left, where there were 250 men. Captain McDonald and Lieutenant Campbell were soon killed, Lieutenant McDonald was wounded at the same time, and our people being overpowered gave way where those officers had been killed. I did all in my power to keep things in order, but to no purpose; the 100 Pennsylvanians who were posted upon the right at the greatest distance from the enemy, went off without orders, without firing a shot; in short, in less than half an hour all was in confusion, and as soon as that happened we were fired upon from every quarter.

I endeavored to rally the troops upon every rising ground, and I did all in my power in that melancholy situation to make the best retreat I could. I sent an officer to Major Lewis to make the best disposition he could with the Americans and Virginians till I could come up, and I was in hopes to be able to make a stand there and at least to make a tolerable retreat. Unfortunately, upon hearing the firing the Major thought the best thing that could be done was to march to our assistance, unluckily they did not take the same road by which I marched the night before and by which they had passed that morning, and as I retired the same way I had advanced, I never saw them when I found Captain Bullet and his fifty men alone. I could not help saying to him that I was undone. However, though there was little or rather no hopes left, I was resolved to do the best I could, and whenever I could get any body to stay with me made a stand, sometimes with 100 and sometimes with 50, just as the men thought proper, for orders were to no purpose. Fear had then got the better of every other passion, and I hope I shall never see again such a pannick among troops—till then I had no conception of it.

At last, inclining to the left with about fifty men, where I was told a number of the Americans and Highlanders had gone, my party diminished insensibly, every soldier taking the road he liked best, and I found myself with not above a dozen of men and an officer of the Pennsylvanians who had been left with Captain Bullet. Surrounded on all sides by the Indians, and when I expected every instant to be cut to pieces, without a possibility of escaping, a body of the French with a number of their officers came up and offered me quarters, which I accepted of. I was then within a short league of the fort; it was then about 11 o'clock, and, as far as I can judge, about that time the French troops were called back and the pursuit ended. What our loss is, you best know, but it must be considerable. Captains McDonald and Munroe, Lieutenants Alex. McKenzie, Collin Campbell and Wm. McKenzie, Lieutenants Rider and Ensign Jenkins and Wollar are prisoners. Ensign J. MacDonald is prisoner with the Indians; from what I hear they have got two other officers, whose names or corps I know not. Mr. Rhor and the officer who conducted the Indians were killed. Major Lewis and Captain McKenzie are prisoners. I am not certain that Lieutenant McKenzie was killed, but I have seen his commission, which makes it very probable. I spoke to Lieutenant McDonald, Senior, after he was wounded, and I think he could hardly make his escape. I wish I may be mistaken. This is the best account I can give you of our unlucky affair. I endeavoured to execute the orders which I had received to the best of my power; as I have been unfortunate, the world may possibly find fault in my conduct. I flatter myself that you will not. I may have committed mistakes without knowing them, but if I was sensible of them I most certainly should tell you in what I thought I had done wrong. I am willing to flatter myself that my being a prisoner will be no detriment to my promotion in case vacancies should happen in the army, and it is to be hoped that the proper steps will be taken to get me exchanged as soon as possible.

I have the honor to be, Sir,

Your most obedient and most humble servant.

P. S.—As Major Lewis is prisoner, I thought it was right to read to him that part of this letter which particularly concerns him. He says when he came back to speak to me, that he gave no orders for the troops to retire from the plain. That Captain Saunder, who was the next officer to him, can best account for that step; for they did retire, and I took it for granted that it was by the Major's orders, till he assured me of the contrary. Mr. Jenkins, of the Americans, is a pretty young lad, and has spirit. He is the oldest ensign, and is much afraid that being a prisoner will be a detriment to his promotion. He begs that I may mention him to you, and I could not think of refusing him.

To George Washington
Letters to Washington, v.3, p.103

Raestown 16 Sept. 1758

Sir,

I have the favor of yours of the 12th. and I am told Mr Rutherford's complaint is occasioned by Col Bouquet's having refused some cattle of Mr Walker's, that really was not fit to be used in our way, and therefore Col B. gave orders not to purchase any more such.

I am extremely obliged to you for your good wishes of recovery which I now really stand in need of, being quite as feeble as a child almost—however here I am and I hope to profit daily—I am sorry to hear my poor friend Cl. Byrd has been very bad. I wish he were able to come here where I should hope to prove a better physician than he will probably meet with at Fort Cumberland. They tell me here that you threaten us with a visit soon, which I should be glad of whenever it happens, being very sincerely

Yr most obedt.

Jo. Fforbes.

To Governor Sharpe
Pennsylvania Magazine, v.33, p.90

Raestown 16th Septemr 1758

Dear Sir

I received your letter from Fort Cumberland at Juniata last night, and that I might answer it more exactly brought your officer on here this day, where I now find there has a transport gone from here this morning for Fort Cumberland with provisions which will serve in the meantime untill Mr Rutherford arrives; what I was to do with regard to spirits I could not well say, imagining they could be bought as reasonable and cheap at Fort Cumberland as they could be sent from this, but now being informed of the contrary I have ordered two hogsheads to be sent off directly, which will give me time to look about me for a day or two and draw Breath, being at this present moment in bed wearied like a dog.

I have the most laconic letter from Dr. Ross that ever was wrote to a Gentleman where £1500. was concerned, consisting of these words. "Sir I have received yours and shall report to Govr Sharp. I am Sir" —In a day or two I hope to write you more fully upon several other things. In the meantime I am very sincerely

Yr most obedt &

Most humle Servt

Jo Fforbes

P. S.—If spirits can be purchased reasonable at Fort Cumberland, I dont see why we should be obliged to send them from this. Mr St. Clair is just now come in and informs me that the transport of provisions above mentioned, did not proceed as I have said—However as there is an Express gone to Winchester to Mr. Rutherford to hasten him up, I hope you will be able to make a shift untill that he arrives or that I can send you a fresh supply, which shall be the first thing I shall take care of when any comes to this place, and that expect tomorrow or the day after

Colonel Bouquet to General Amherst

Darlington's Fort Pitt and letters from the frontier, p.75

Loyal Hanna, Sept. 17, 1758.

Camp at Loyal Hanna, Sept. 17, 1758.

Sir:—In the situation in which you are, sick, etc., it is with double regret, that I must inform you of the misfortune which has happened to Major Grant, who after a long engagement has been defeated on the 14th current.

I do not make any apology for the part which I took in this affair. I leave the detail of facts to condemn or justify me.

The day on which I arrived at the camp, which was the 7th, it was reported to me that we were surrounded by parties of Indians, several soldiers having been scalped, or made prisoners.

Being obliged to have our cattle and our horses in the woods, our people could not guard or search for them, without being continually liable to fall into the hands of the enemy.

Lieutenant Col. Dagworthy and our Indians not having yet arrived, I ordered two companies each of a hundred men to occupy the path ways and try to cut off the enemies in their ambush and release our prisoners. These detachments being ready to march, Major Grant drew me aside and said that he was surprised that I took this method, after so many proofs that these little parties never did anything, and

served to lose our men and discourage our people; but if I would give
him five hundred men, he would go to the fort, reconnoitre the roads
and the forces of the enemy, which according to all our reports does
not exceed six hundred French and Indians, that this was confirmed
by a party which had entered the town, and that whatever detachments they could make, they could not send out more than they have,
and that by erecting an ambuscade he could take prisoners.

I made some objection to letting him go, but he insisted, and in-
fluenced by his reasons and the situation in which we found ourselves I consented and countermanded the two parties who were under
arms.   Having sent for Col. Burd and Major Lewis (Lieut. Col.
Stephen being under arrest I told his Major to inform him of the
affair), I informed these gentlemen of the proposition made by Major
Grant to procure for us sure intelligence which would give us some
advantage over the Indians, who insulted us every day with impunity,
and that this would be the way to cure our men of the fear which
they had of them.   Those who had escaped from their attacks had
thrown down their arms that they might fly faster.

I begged them to give me their opinion upon a project of which
I had several times spoken to Major Grant at Raystown, which was
to attack during the night the Indians who camped around the Fort
in huts, and that the disposition could be made thus: Lieutenant-
Colonel Dagworthy (who should arrive this evening or to-morrow with
the Indians) should march with 900 men to the post, which was known
to be 10 miles distant, there construct an entrenchment and remain
with 200 men.   The Major should march with 300 Highlanders, 100
R. A., 150 Virginians, 100 Marylanders and 100 Pennsyia, and all the
Indians to the neighborhood of the fort, regulating their march so
as to be five miles from the fort in the evening, with the precautions
necessary to prevent a surprise; and from there he would send the
Indians and such of the officers as knew the environs of the place to
reconnoitre, and if he found by the appearance of the enemy that he
had not been discovered, he would advance on the hill, half a mile
from the fort, when he would reconnoitre himself the fires of the
Indians and make his arrangements accordingly.   In case he saw them
around their fires, he should send parties of his detachment with white
shirts over their clothes to attack them soon after midnight, the
bayonets on the guns and only fire in extremity, it not being difficult
to surprise them, as they do not keep sentinels.   This *coup*, made or
missed, he should beat a retreat to the height, where they should stop
with the rest of the troops and the Indians, and as soon as his
people, directed by the sound, should have joined him, he should immediately retire six miles from the fort before day, and there form an
ambuscade of all his men and the Indians, in case the enemy should
follow leaving a small company round the post to observe their movements and inform him of them.   If he should conquer them at the
ambuscade he could then return safely to the fort to take a plan

of it and reconnoitre the environs. But if by his spies or himself he finds that he was discovered, he should only think of retiring. This is the plan that was proposed, and to execute it preparations were made the next day.

On the 9th he departed, and I joined him on the 10th at the post, where Lieutenant-Colonel Dagworthy should have stopped. I remained here all night and saw him depart on the 11th with his detachment in good order. This post being nearly ready for defence, I returned to the camp. Instead of this plan, which did not compel him to fight, or which gave him in that case every advantage of disposition, and choice of ground with all his troops together, here is what he appears to have done: Having arrived at the height only one fire was seen, but Ensign Chew, who had reconnoitered, said that all the Indians lay in the block houses, which were easy to force. He sent there Major Lewis with 400 men; some confusion being among the troops he feared he had been discovered and returned to Major Grant, who sent there at once two companies of Highlanders. They visited the block houses, but found no one. They put out the fire and returned. The Major, according to his orders, should have retired, but unfortunately he thought that the garrison was too weak to dare risk a sortie, and in consequence he remained on the height untill morning. He then beat the *reveille* in different places, and ordered Major Lewis to place himself in ambuscade with the baggage and 100 R. A., 150 Virginians, 200 Highlanders, 100 'Maryl' and 100 Penns. were placed on the heights, and he sent Captain McDonald with 100 Highlanders, drums beating, straight to the fort. Some one had seen a party leave the garrison as though they would cut off the retreat. Hardly had McDonald gone half the distance, when he heard the whoop of the Indians, followed immediately by a sortie of nearly 300 French and Indians, who fell upon them. He killed so many of these people at his first fire that they turned aside and surrounded him. He pierced through them, where he was killed. The companies of Monro and McKenzie, who desended to their assistance, were put in disorder and the Captain killed. As the enemy continually received reinforcements, all the troops were soon engaged, and the fire sustained a long time after our men yielded. Major Lewis, who was distant about two miles, heard the firing, urged by his officers and the soldiers, quit his post to go to their assistance. He arrived just at the moment our men retired in disorder towards his post. He had gained a height which had put his men out of breath, and, stopping, they found themselves under fire of the enemy. The action was, nevertheless, still very lively and for a long time disputed. At last our men yielded, and there remained only a scene of confusion, notwithstanding all the efforts of Major Grant to rally them. They would have been cut to pieces probably had not Captain Bullet of the Virginians, with 100 men, sustained the combat with all their power, until, having lost two-thirds of his men, he was driven to the

shore of the river, where he found the poor Major. He urged him
to retire, but he said he would not quit the field of battle as long
as there was a man who would fight. My heart is broke (said he)
I shall never outlive this day. They were soon surrounded, and the
Frenchmen, calling him by his name, offered quarter. He would not
accept it. They would not fire on him, wishing to take him prisoner.
Captain Bullet continued firing. At last they also fired and drove
his party into the Ohio, where a great number were drowned. Bullet
escaped, but I have no news of the Major.

At the first news of his misfortune I sent Lieutenant-Colonel
Stephen with 300 men to join Lieutenant-Colonel Dagworthy to cover
their retreat. The Indians did not pursue them far. Our post misses
some officers and it lacks yet 270 men. Many have crossed the river,
and it is thought many will escape. Our Catawbas did not fire and
the Tuscararas and Nottaways did very well.

It appears from the testimony of the Indians and of our men that
the French have lost many men, mostly Indians. The French did not
try to kill but to make prisoners, and it seems for the first time they
shewed humanity, which makes me hope that the Major and several
others of the officers whom we miss are saved.

I have written to Colonel Washington to march to Rays Town,
leaving 100 men at Cumberland, until the arrival of the militia of
Maryland. This reinforcement is necessary to secure to our convoys
communication. Contrary to my expectations the troops do not appear
depressed by this check, and if all was ready elsewhere, they would
be more ready than ever to go to the front. Reports of an action in
the woods are so confused that I cannot render you an exact account
of what happened there, but I will send to you an officer as soon
as I know what is best to do. Many of the arms are broken, some
lost. We must have others to replace them. We are assured that the
Delawares and the Shawnees were against us, and among the men
taken and scalped around the camp is a German who came, it is
said, from Ohio, and who, I suppose, was sent by the Governor of
Pennsylvania. The enemy had received a considerable reinforcement
the evening of the action. The account of their number varies from
3000 to 1200. There was discovered on the island a camp of more
than 100 tents. For the state of the roads and the fort I refer you
to the report which the officer will deliver to you. The post is much
more considerable than we had thought and many new works have
been added. We have not seen an Indian for eight days, we think
that after this success it will be difficult for the French to keep them.
I will send a letter to the Governor to make known the fate of those
who are missing.

The Provincials appear to have done well and their good men
are better in this war than the regular troops.

I will not add any reflections on this affair, they are too unpleasant. If the French wish to attack us in their turn, we will be in two days ready to receive them, being all reunited at this post.

I have the honor, to be, Sir,

Your very obedt. servant,

Henry Bouquet

To Colonel Bouquet

Darlington's Fort Pitt and letters from the frontier, p.71

Raestown, September 23, 1758.

Sir:—Your letter of the 17th, from Loyal Hanning, I read with no less surprise than real concern, as indeed I could not well believe that such an attempt would have been carried into execution without my previous knowledge and concurrence, as you well know my opinion, and dread of the consequences of running any risque of the troops meeting with the smallest check. As well as my fears of alienating and altering the disposition of the Indians, at this critical time, who (tho' fickle and wavering), yet were seemingly well disposed to embrace our alliance and protection. But I need not recapitulate to you my many good reasons against any attempt of this kind being made at this time; nor repeat to you how happy your assurances made me, of all my orders and directions having been (and would be) complyed with. For which I rested secure, and plumed myself in our good fortune, in having the head of our army advanced, as it were, to the beard of the enemy, and secured in a good post well guarded and cautioned against surprise. Our roads almost completed; our provisions all upon wheels, and all this without any loss on our side, and our small army all ready to join and act in a collected body whenever we pleased to attack the enemy, or that any favourable opportunity presented itself to us.

Thus the breaking in upon—not to say disappointments of—our hitherto so fair and flattering hopes of success touches most sensibly. How far we shall find the bad effects of it, I shall not pretend to say. At present I shall suspend judging, altho' I have languished for the officer you promised to send me down—whom I have expected hourly —and a letter from you of your present situation, with the state of the posts, and the strength at them, that the escorts may be proportioned. I acquainted you of the state of our provisions, and the hopes I have of being immediately supplied with 1,000 barrels of pork and at least 1,200 barrels of flour, all of which, by this time, is actually upon its march, and will arrive here daily. So, I shall forward it as fast as I can, altho' large convoys and escorts are very inconvenient. The description of the roads is so various and disagreeable that I do not know what to think or say. Lieutenant Evans came down here the other day, and described the Laurell Hill as, at present, impracticable, but said he could mend it with the assistance of 500 men, fascines and fagots, in one day's time.

Col. Stephens writes Col. Washington that he is told by everybody that the road from Loyal Hannon to the Ohio and the French fort is now impracticable. For what reason, or why, he writes thus I do not know; but I see Col. Washington and my friend, Col. Byrd, would rather be glad this was true than otherways, seeing the other road (their favourite scheme) was not followed out. I told them plainly that, whatever they thought, yet I did aver that, in our prosecuting the present road, we had proceeded from the best intelligence that could be got for the good and convenience of the army, without any views to oblige any one province or another; and added that those two gentlemen were the only people that I had met with who had shewed their weakness in their attachment to the province they belong to, by declaring so publickly in favour of one road without their knowing anything of the other, having never heard from any Pennsylvania person one word about the road; and that, as for myself, I could safely say—and believed I might answer for you—that the good of the service was the only view we had at heart, not valuing the provincial interest, jealousys, or suspicions, one single twopence; and that, therefore, I could not believe Col. Stephen's descriptions untill I had heard from you, which I hope you will very soon be able to disprove.

I fancy what I said more on this subject will cure them from coming upon this topic again. However, I beg you will cause look into the Laurell Hill, and let it be set to rights as fast as possible; and let all the different posts, and the different convoys and escorts, as they pass along, repair the bad steps, and keep the roads already made in constant order.

I have sent Mr. Basset back the length of Fort Loudoun, in order to divide the troops from thence to Juniata, in small partys, all along that road, who are to set it all to rights, and keep it so; and as the partys are all encamped within five or six miles one of another, they serve as escorts to the provisions and forage that is coming up, at the same time. I am extreamly sorry for your loss of De Rhorr; nor can I well conceive what I had to do there. Mr. Gordon, who, it seems, had the direction of the works here, left this without leaving the plan or sketch of this place or environs, or leaving any directions, as far as I can yet learn, either with the people employed to carry the general plan into execution, or how that they were further to proceed; and, notwithstanding the multiplicity of working-tools, I am at a loss to find a sufficient number for helping the roads and clearing the stumps or other impediments about the camp; nor can I well imagine what is become of all the rest.

There are two wounded Highland officers just now arriv'd, who give so lame an account of how matters proceeded, or any kind of description of the ground, that one can draw nothing from them—only that my friend Grant had most certainly lost the *tra mon tane*, and by his thirst of fame, brought on his own perdition, and run a great

risque of ours, which was far wide of the promises he made me at
Carlisle, when soliciting to command a party, which I would not agree
to; and, very contrary to his criticisms upon Gen. Abercromby's late
affair, has unhappily fallen into the individual same error, by his
inconsiderate and rash proceeding.

I understand by these officers that you have withdrawn the troops
from your advanced post, which I attribute to its being too small for
what you intended it, or that it did not answer the strength that you
at first described it to me. I shall be glad to hear all your people are
in spirits, and keep so, and that Loyall Hannon will be soon past any
insult without cannon. I shall be soon afraid to crowd you with provisions, nor would I wish to crowd the troops any faster up, untill our
magazines are thoroughly formed, if you have enough of troops for
your own defence and compleating the roads; and I see the absolute
necessity there is for my stay here some days, in order to carry on the
transport of provisions and forage, which, without my constant attention, would fail directly. The road forward to the Ohio must be reconnoitered again in order to be sure of our further progress, for it
would grieve me sadly that Mr. Washington or Mr. Byrd should have
any reason to find fault with that, which without their knowledge they
have so publickly exclaimed against. When you have settled things
to your mind, I beg you will write me, and as soon as you conveniently
can, come down, were it only for a day, and if Colonel Armstrong
could be spared, should be glad he came along, in order to settle our
further proceedings, and to seize the first favourable opportunity of
marching directly forwards. The artillery that is left here I would
march in two divisions to prevent a long train of waggons, and the
tearing up the roads. The Congress at Eastown had the most favourable appearance, as there was 500 Indians already come in, but what
they will now do, God knows. Pray make up a hovell or hutt for me
at L. Hannon or any other of the posts with a fire place if possible.
Sir John St. Clair says that if I say he was in the wrong to Colonel
Stevens, he will readily acknowledge it. I do not choose meddling,
but I think Colonel Stevens might act, and trust to Sir John's ac-
knowledgment.

> I am, dear sir,
> Your most obedient servant,
> Jo. Forbes.

To Governor Sharpe

Archives of Maryland, v.9, p.274

Sir

I am this moment favour'd with yours and am very much obliged
to you, for the Care you have taken of our good Fort Cumberland,
this will be deliverd you by Mr Clerk, whom I had sent over on purpose to settle matters with regard to provisions &c, So whatever you

have wanted or may want he will settle with you as you shall please
to direct,   as to the Virginia complaint I thought it frivilous and
triffling from the beginning, you can easily see I was obliged to take
notice of it, on purpose to please.   I shall send of an Escort tomorrow for the Waggons, but if the Escort of Coll⁰ Byrds Regᵗ is not yet
come away, they may Stay and Come along with the Waggons, or
Escort them till they meet the Party I send off tomorrow.   As there
will be some empty waggons, I shall expect the Spare wheel Carriage
that Major Halket wrote about.   As I understand you have some
Garden Stuff such as Cabbage &c. I beg you will be so good as ordʳ
some to be sent over here by the Waggons.   I am

My Dʳ Sir
Your most obdᵗ humble Servᵗ
Jo. fforbes

Raes Camp Octobʳ 5th 1758.

Excuse another hand having been unable to write myself these ten
days.

Unsigned letter from the "Pennsylvania gazette," Oct. 12, 1758,
describing Grant's defeat
Olden time, v.1, p.179

Annapolis, October 5th, 1758.

We are informed by a letter from Frederick county, that on Mon-
day, the 11th of September, Maj. Grant, of the Highland regiment,
marched from our camp on the waters of the Kiskiminitas, with 37
officers and 805 privates, taken from the different regiments that
compose the Western Army, on an expedition against Fort Duquesne.

The third day after their march, they arrived within eleven miles
of Fort Duquesne, and halted till three o'clock in the afternoon; then
marched within two miles of Fort Duquesne, and left their baggage
there, guarded by a captain, two subalterns, and fifty men, and
marched with the rest of the troops, and arrived at eleven o'clock at
night upon a hill, a quarter of a mile from the fort.   Maj. Grant
sent two officers and fifty men to the fort, to attack all the Indians,
&c., they should find lying out of the fort; they saw none, nor were
they challenged by the centries.   As they returned, they set fire to
a large store house, which was put out as soon as they left it.   At
break of day, Major Lewis was sent with 200 men, (royal Americans
and Virginians,) to lie in ambush a mile and a half from the main
body, on the path on which they left their baggage, imagining the
French would send to attack the baggage guard and seize it.   Four
hundred men were posted along the hill facing the fort, to cover the
retreat of Capt. M'Donald's company, who marched with drums beating toward the fort, in order to draw a party out of the fort, as
Maj. Grant had some reason to believe there were not above 200 men
in the fort, including Indians; but as soon as they heard the drums,

they sallied out in great numbers, both French and Indians, and fell upon Captain M'Donald, and two columns that were posted lower on the hill to receive them. The Highlanders exposed themselves without any cover, and were shot down in great numbers, and soon forced to retreat. The Carolinians, Marylanders, and Lower Countrymen, concealing themselves behind trees and the brush, made a good defence; but were overpowered by numbers, and not being supported, were obliged to follow the rest. Maj. Grant exposed himself in the thickest of the fire, and endeavored to rally his men, but all to no purpose, as they were by this time flanked on all sides. Major Lewis and his party came up and engaged, but were soon obliged to give way, the enemy having the hill of him, and flanking him every way. A number were drove into the Ohio, most of whom were drowned. Major Grant retreated to the baggage, where Captain Bullet was posted with fifty men, and again endeavored to rally the flying soldiers, by entreating them in the most pathetic manner to stand by him, but all in vain, as the enemy were close at their heels. As soon as the enemy came up to Captain Bullet, he attacked them very furiously for some time, but not being supported, and most of his men killed, was obliged to give way. However, his attacking them stopped the pursuit, so as to give many an opportunity of escaping. The enemy followed Major Grant, and at last separated them, and Captain Bullet was obliged to make off. He imagines the Major must be taken, as he was surrounded on all sides, but the enemy would not kill him, and often called to him to surrender. The French gave quarters to all that would accept it.

Colonel Burd to Colonel Bouquet

Darlington's Fort Pitt and letters from the frontier, p.81

Camp at Loyal Hannon, October 12, 1758.

To Col. Bouquet at Stoney Creek on the Laurell Hill:

Dear Sir:—I had the pleasure to receive your favours of this date this evening at 7 P. M. I shall be glad to see you. I send you, through Lieut.-Coll. Lloyd (who marches to you with 200 men), the 100 falling axes, etc., you desire.

This day, at 11 A. M., the enemy fired twelve guns to the southwest of us, upon which I sent out two partys to surround them; but instantly the firing increased, upon which I sent out a larger party of 500 men. They were forced to the camp, and immediately a regular attack ensued, which lasted a long time; I think about two hours. But we had the pleasure to do that honour to his majesty's arms, to keep his camp at Loyal Hannon. I can't inform you of our loss, nor that of the enemy. Must refer you for the particulars to Lieut.-Col. Lloyd. One of their soldiers, which we have mortally wounded, says they were 1200 strong and 200 Indians, but I can ascertain nothing of this further. I have drove them off the field; but I don't doubt of a second attack. If they do I am ready.

Being most sincerely,

My dear sir,

Your most sincere friend and

Obe't humble serv't,

James Burd

[Since writing we have been fired upon.]

Col. Bouquet.

Letter of Colonel Bouquet

(The address torn away all but the word "Rays Town.")

Darlington's Fort Pitt and letters from the frontier, p.82

Rays Dudgeon, October 13, 1758, 10 P. M.

Sir:—After having written to you this morning, I went to reconnoitre Laurell Hill, with a party of eighty men, some firing of guns around us made me suspect that it was the signal of an enemy's party. I sent to find out, and one of our party having perceived the Indians, fired on them. We continued our march and have found a very good road for ascending the mountain, although very stony in two places. The old road is absolutely impracticable.

I have had this afternoon a second letter from Colonel Burd. The enemies have been all night around the entrenchments, and have made several false attacks. The cannon and the cohortes have held them in awe, and until the Colonel had sent to reconnoitre the environs, he was not sure that they had retired. At this moment is heard from the mountains several cannon shots which makes me judge that the enemies have not yet abandoned the party, and at all events I am going to attempt to re-enter this post before day. The 200 men which Colonel Burd sent to me, have eaten nothing for two days. I received this moment provisions from Stoney Creek, and will depart in two hours.

I have not got any report of our loss, two officers from Maryland have been killed, and one wounded. Duncannon of Virginia mortally wounded, also one officer of the first Battalion of Pennsylvania, and nearly fifty men.

The loss of the enemy must be considerable to judge by the reports of our men and the fire which they have clearly wasted. Without this cursed rain we would have arrived in time with the artillery and 200 men, and I believe it would have made a difference.

As soon as it is possible, I will send you word how we are. Be at rest about the post. I have left it in a state to defend itself against all attacks without cannon, and I learn that they have finished all that remains to be done.

I am with entire devotion, Sir,

Your very humble and very obedient servant,

Henry Bouquet.

To Richard Peters

Pennsylvania Magazine, v.33, p.91

Sir

I have been of late but a bad correspondent as I could only write of multiplicity of grievances crowding upon the back of one another, all dismall to look at, yet by patience and perseverance, to be in some measure surmounted or alleviate. This I hope in God I have done, and trust greatly that from the same principles I shall be able to accomplish what yet remains.

I wish sincerely your treaty could have been brought about a little earlier, from whence wee might have drawn some powerfull helps this very Campaign, but I never repine at what cannot be remedyed, and I am this moment flattering myself that from the joint endeavours of all with you, the dropping of foolish trifles, some measures will be taken with those originale Inhabitants as to strengthen ourselves and diminish our Ennemys Influence with them in those parts for if it is as I see things giving up sometimes a little in the beginning will procure you a great deal in the end.

Frederick Post has been here some time, I think he has execute the Commission he was sent upon, wth ability and Fidelity, and deserves a proper reward. The two people who reconducted him here, deserve likewise of any Government, but I think if what he says of Daniell be true that he deserves no countenance. I do not know whether the province will defray those charges, but they certainly ought as they may reap the profitts, I have no kind of judgment what Post deserves. I have ordered him fifteen pounds in the mean time I send him to you by this Express, that he and his two Conductors may be sent directly back with proper Messages (as the Governor shall direct) to the Ohio Indians to retire directly, as the season will admitt of no delay.

Pray make my excuse to Mr. Croghan for not answering his letter, but I approve of his measures and proposall of joining me, which I wish he would do without the loss of one moment of time, as now that I have everything in readyness at Loyall Hannon, I only want a few dry days to carry me to the Ohio Banks, where I hope our operations will not be long, so send me back the express that carrys this, with all diligence and let Mr. Croghan write me the day that he intends setting out, with his route, and when I may expect him here, with the number that he expects to accompany him, Dispatch at present is absolutely necessary, so I should think he can dispense without seeing the end of your Congress.

Most of the Indians that have been preying upon us all year, have after getting all they possibly could expect, left us, and the few remaining were just agoing home in spite of every kind of means used to prevent them, when the little Carpenter arrived at this Camp with about 60 good Warriors, But he is as consummate a Dog as any of them, only seeing our distress, has made him exceed all others in his most avaricious demands, There is no help for those criticall minutes, and after foolishly laying out many thousands of pounds, I judged it would be wrong policy to lose him and all the rest for a few hundreds more.

Upon the 12th in the morning the French from Fort Du Quesne having a mind to repay Major Grants visit came to drive us away from our advanced post at Loyall Hannon destroy our Magazin, Bullocks, Carriages, &ce. They consisted of a body of 900 French and Canadians and two Hundred of those Friends, you are now treating with, they had gott within five miles of the post, and proposed attacking all the out post and Guards next morning, but being discovered they resolutely attempted to storm the Breast work thrown up about the Camp—accordingly fell a firing and Hallooing in order to bring out detachments, by which they proposed entering the Breastwork pell mell with them when routed. The 60 Maryland Volunteers went out and attacked them with vigour and Courage, but overpowered, Col. Burd who commanded sent a strong detatchment of the 1st Pensylvania Regt to sustain them, but they being likewise repulsed a third detatchment of the Virginians &c, went out to bring the other off, which they did by retreating to the Breastwork. The Ennemy followed closs to the edge of the Wood where they were stopt by the Grape shot from our Cannon and the shells of the Coehorns and Howbitzers, however they continued fireing upon the breast work from eleven to three in the afternoon without any Considerable loss on our side, they then retreated a little, and carried away their dead and wounded in which they were favoured by the lying of the Ground, and then marched five miles off. Wee saved all our live Cattle, but the officers horses are either carried away or a missing. Two Maryland officers are killed and about 60 of our men are missing altho wee cannot believe them killed having only found six bodys, one officer of the Train wounded, wch is all our loss. That of the Ennemy wee cannot ascertain, altho it must neads be Considerable considering the advantages wee fought with against them, a Breast work & Cannon—I fancy they will not visit soon again and it has put all the Waggoners in such spirits that a single waggon will go now without one escorte, but these cursed Rains upon our new roads in clay soils and everything upon wheels, has at present renderd the Laurell Hill quite unpassable so wee must wait some dry days to be able to go forward. God grant them soon—

I think Mr. Croghan might send a trusty man or two or three towards Venango, in a direct Road from you, who by coming down the Ohio might come over and join us at Loyal Hannon with what intelligence of the Reinforcements lately gone to the French they could pick up, and what tribes of Indians are still with them which sure can not be many now as I am sure they are scarce of provisions. Pray make my apology to Govr Denny for not writing him, being still extreamely bad that is to say, weak, and my Complim^{ts} to him and Govr Bernard, to whose negotiations, I sincerely wish success, and hope they cannot fail, send me all your news by the express and believe me Sir very sincerely

Yr most ob^t hum^{le} Servt

Jo Fforbes

Raystown Camp

October 16th

Pray heartily for fair weather and dispatch of Business—But what absurd mortall made your Assembly settle the price of transporting provisions this length and no further— This length the Waggons do come & finer horses and Waggons I never saw, each bringing at least 2000 Weight with ease, but one foot further they will not move, so I am drove to the necessity of persuading them to move forward in the military way, but still paying them in proportion, or leaving the price to their Assembly—I am quite tyred. Adieu. I have sent home your books.

To William Pitt

Correspondence of William Pitt with colonial governors in America, v.1, p.370.

Raes Town Camp. 20th Octob^r. 1758.

Sir

. . .I acquainted you of Major Grant of Col^o. Montgomery's Battalion with a strong detachment of 900 men, having gone to Fort Du Quesne in order to reconnoitre the roads & Fort, to check the Enemy's scouting partys and to endeavour to make some Prisoners in order to get some Intelligence of the Enemy's Strength, &c^a., which, in spite of all my Endeavours to learn, by every Means That I could devize we are still in the dark off, as to the certainty of their Numbers.

Major Grant trusting to false reports of their strength, divided his troops in order to bring them into an ambuscade, and at break of Day, beat his Drums and discovered himself to the Fort, who immediately poured out a large Body of Men, attacked his divided troops one after another, never allowing him time to get them together, and consequently had no difficult task in totally dispersing of him.

The Majors Grant and Lewis of the Virginia Provincialls were mad prisoners with 4 more officers, seven officers killed and 270 Private Men. This was a most terrible check to my small Army, at that time (the 14 September) just got in readiness to have marched to the Enemy, as to our Men, had the roads, provisions for man and horse, and the other absolute necessarys corresponded, as it raised the

Enemy's Spirits and depressed our's, and at that Critical time was of great consequence, as it run a risque of rivetting the Indians to their Interest, who were then fluctuating betwixt the sides that they were to choose, and who I then verily believed were upon the point of returning to their old habitations upon the Susquehannah, and declaring for us.

For which reason I had Some time before that, suspended all military Operations against them and their villages, in hopes of gaining them entirely to our Interest, which I hope is now in a great Measure done, in a sollemn meeting with their Chieffs at Easton upon the Dellaware, where we have gott the Governours of Pennsylvania and Jersey to attend them, but as yet I do not know the result of their deliberations.

Since then nothing has happened, except that upon the 12th.. Inst. a Body of 900 French & Canadians, came to repay Major Grant's visit, and to attack our furthest advanced post at Loyal Hannon, which if they did not carry, they were to destroy our Baggage Horses and the live Cattle for our Subsistance. They attacked the Post for three hours, with little damage on either side, as our men were both more numerous, covered with a good Breastwork, and had two small Redoubts, and five piece of Cannon and Cohorns that played upon the Enemy.

They retreated in the Evening after burying their killed except a very few, and carrying off their wounded, so I do not know their loss, ours were two Maryland officers, and about 60 Men killed and missing, of which last severals have come in since, having been lost in the woods.

They carried off all the Baggage Horses belonging to that post, but we saved all our Oxen, I was extreamly angry to find our people had not pursued and attacked their rear in their retreat, from which we might have made reprizalls, but as our troops were mostly provincialls, I was obliged to attribute it to their ignorance, for to do justice I must commend the spirit of some of the provincialls, particularly the Maryland troops, who I retained in the Service, after being left to disband by their Province, and therefore I was obliged to keep them together on our pay, and have been necesitated to advance them from time to time, money for their support, and cloathing, to enable them to carry on the Service, and without which they must have left us, as they had no manner of cloathing but one bad blankett each, which will not do in these cold evenings and mornings, no shoes stockings or Breeches, or any one necessary against the Inclemency of the Weather.

The Cherokee and other Southern Indians who came last winter, and so early in the Spring to join us, after having by every Art they were Masters off, gott every thing they could expect from us, left us without any remorse when they found they were not likely to get any more presents for retaining them, so that I have not now left with me above fifty, and I am now upon my march to the Ohio, as the Season will not admitt of one Moment's delay, and I wish most sincerely I could have proceeded sooner, as I have no alternative left me now, but a bold push at last, to which I have been absolutely drove by a Multiplicity of Cross Events, too long to trouble you with at present; but the principal reasons that retarded us after gathering our troops together, was the Waggon-Horses failing in bringing up our Provisions, neither making proper journeys, nor carrying the stipulated weight, by which the Magazines (upon the faith and strength of which I was to have proceeded) diminished daily, nor is it easy to replenish them, or support the daily Consumption of an Army, 300 miles distance, and that all land Carriage. The 2^d. was the roads, first over the Alleganey Mountains, and then over the Laurell Hills, that are worse. The whole an immense uninhabited Wilderness overgrown every where with trees and underbrush, so that no where can anyone see twenty yards, those roads during the hott and dry Seasons were made practicable for carriages, and I was assured by every one, and made believe that the Months of October and November were the two best Months in the year for an Expedition, because of the trees losing their leaves, by which one can see a little thro' the woods, and prevent the Enemy's surprizes, which is their only strength, and likewise, that in those two Months the Indians leave the French as it is their chief hunting Season, in which they provide for their familys during the winter.

This last was of great consequence to me, as the Enemy's Numbers had all along been represented to me, not only equall, but even to exceed what I could carry against them, so it was absolutely necessary that I should take precautions by having posts along my route, which I have done from a project that I took from *Turpin's Essay Sur la Guerre*. Last Chaptre 4th. Book. Intitled *Principe Sur lequel on peut etabler un projet de Campagne*, if you will take the trouble of looking into his Book, you will see the Generall principles upon which I have proceeded.

I am this Moment in the greatest distress, occasioned by unusuall rains at this Season, which joined to our Number of Carriages have rendered the clay roads absolutely impracticable to our Artillery and Waggons. As the Horses are a good deal wore out, I still hope a few days will make a change and enable me to proceed; If the Weather does not favour, I shall be absolutely locked up in the Mountains, nor do I scarce see a possibility of recrossing the Alleganey Mountain. This I could not foresee, nor prevent, as it is quite uncommon here.

I have therefore sent to Virginia, Pensylvania, and Maryland, begging to know what Troops they will furnish me, during the Winter, for the Protection of their Frontiers & Garrisoning the posts and footing we have got so nigh the Enemy, representing to them the small number of regulars I have (not above 1200 Men) and how unequal to such a task. But as all their troops are only engaged to the beginning of December, I dread the dilatory procedure of their Assemblys will not answer my peremptory Demands of their Aid, at this perplexing juncture for me.

I cannot form any judgment, how I am to extricate myself, as every thing depends upon the Weather, which snows and rains frightfully, but I shall do myself the honour of writing you every step I take, which to the Utmost of my weak abilities, shall be for the best. I have this Moment an Express from the treaty with the Ohio Indians at Easton, who have promised to join us, but require time, a thing at present so precious to me, that I have none to spare, and must in a day or two choose either to risque every thing, and march to the Enemy's Fort, retreat across the Alleganey if the provincialls leave me, or maintain myself where I am to the Spring.

I have the honour to be with the greatest regard & Esteem Sir
Y^r most Obed^t. & most hum^{le}. Servt.

Jo: Forbes.

Camp Top of the Alleganey Mountains.   October 27th.
Most of the above letter was wrote some days ago, but finding the weather did not mend, I thought it necessary to march forward, to be ready to embrace the first opportunity.

To Governor Denny
Pennsylvania Colonial records, v.8, p.224

Raystown Camp, October 22d, 1758.
Sir:

The Heavy Rains that have fallen of late has rendered the Roads almost Impassable for Carriages; these few Days past of dry Weather have given things a more favourable Aspect, and every thing is in Motion, the last Division being to March from hence to-morrow.

My State of Health continues precarious, but not so bad as to occasion any stop to our Operations, which must now come to a speedy Conclusion on account of the Advanced Season of the year.

Whatever the Fate of the Army may be it is impossible to foresee, but whether we are successful or not it is necessary for me to leave as large and extensive a Barrier as possible to cover the Province of Pennsylvania.

The Number of the King's Troops that I have under my Command does not exceed Twelve Hundred Men, the greatest part of which I must send down to the Inhabited Parts of the Country to recruit and fit themselves out for the ensuing Campaign; for were I to leave the whole during the Winter in the uninhabited parts of the Country, these Corps would not be in a Condition to march on Service early in the Spring.

I shall lay before you the Posts that are proposed to be kept up, which are now in possession of us, leaving it to you and the Assembly of your Province to judge of their Importance to them, and to know how far they can contribute in Men and Expences for the Supporting of these Posts, and making the Soldiers' Lives comfortable, without which no real Service can be expected from them.

I have received no Answer from you relating to Fort Duquesne, if it should please God to grant Success; but whether that Fort is taken or not, the Forts of Loyal Hannon, Cumberland, Raystown, Juniata, Littleton, Loudoun, Frederick, Shippensburgh and Carlisle, ought to be Garrisoned, beside those on the other Side of the Susquehannah. I have wrote to Mr. Fouquiere to know what assistance I may have from the Colony of Virginia, which I do not expect will be very great, not even to Garrison Fort Cumberland, their Frontiers are so extensive that Augusta County will require Two Hundred Men to Garrison its Forts; Winchester, with the south Branch of Potomack, Three Hundred Men more, to which Colonel Washington's Regiment will not amount at the End of the Campaign. I have nothing to expect from Maryland, as I am told they have abandoned Fort Cumberland and Fort Frederick.

It will easily occur to you the Things that will be necessary for making the Soldiers' Lives Comfortable in this severe Climate during the Winter. The most necessary are, a second Blanket in lieu of a bed, a Flannel Jacket, a new pair of Breeches, two Pair of Stockings, and a pair of Shoes.

I should be glad to know, without Loss of Time, how far your Assembly will go in putting it in my power to maintain the Ground that is Gained. If they do nothing for the Safety of the Province, I am certain it is not in my Power to defend them during the Winter with the strength that I shall have left and which I must expect will daily diminish.

To Cover the Country between Susquehannah and Potomack, and to secure the Communication to the advanced Posts will require, in my Opinion, Twelve Hundred Men, stationed in the following manner, Vizt:

At Loyal Hannon	300
At Ray's Town	200
At Fort Cumberland	200
At Fort Frederick	100
At Juniata	100
At Littleton	100
At Loudoun	100
At Shippensburg and Carlisle	100
	1,200 Men

I must intreat you to return me an Answer to this Letter as soon as possible, as it is a Matter of the greatest Consequence to the Colonies.

I am, with the greatest Regard, Sir,
    Your most Obedient and Hume. Servant,

                                            John Forbes.

To the Shawanese and Delawares on the Ohio
Olden Time, v.1, p.161

Brethren, I embrace this opportunity by our brother, *Pesquitomen*, who is now on his return home with some of your uncles, of the *Six Nations*, from the treaty of *Easton*, of giving you joy of the happy conclusion of that great council, which is perfectly agreeable to me; as it is for the mutual advantage of our brethren, the *Indians*, as well as the *English* nation.

I am glad to find that all past disputes and animosities are now finally settled, and amicably adjusted; and I hope they will be for ever buried in oblivion, and that you will now again be firmly united in the interest of your brethren, the *English*.

As I am now advancing, at the head of a large army, against his majesty's enemies, the *French*, on the *Ohio*, I must strongly recommend to you to send immediate notice to any of your people, who may be at the *French* fort, to return forthwith to your towns; where you may sit by your fires, with your wives and children, quiet and undisturbed, and smoke your pipes in safety. Let the *French* fight their own battles, as they were the first cause of the war, and the occasion of the long difference, which hath subsisted between you and your brethren, the *English*; but I must entreat you to restrain your young men from crossing the *Ohio*, as it will be impossible for me to distinguish them from our enemies; which I expect you will comply with, without delay; lest, by your neglect thereof, I should be the innocent cause of some of our brethren's death. This advice take and keep in your own breasts, and suffer it not to reach the ears of the *French*.

As a proof of the truth and sincerity of what I say, and to confirm the tender regard I have for the lives and welfare of our brethren, on the *Ohio*, I send you this string of wampum.

I am, brethren and warriors,
    Your friend and brother,

                                            John Forbes.
[Nov. 9, 1758]?

To Kings Beaver and Shingas
Olden Time, v.1, p.162

Brethren, kings *Beaver* and *Shingas*, and all the warriors, who join with you:

The many acts of hostility, committed by the *French* against the *British* subjects, made it necessary for the king to take up arms, in their defence, and to redress their wrongs, which have been done them; heaven hath favoured the justice of the cause, and given success to his fleets and armies, in different parts of the world. I have received his commands, with regard to what is to be done on the *Ohio*, and shall endeavour to act like a soldier by driving the *French* from thence, or destroying them.

It is a particular pleasure to me to learn, that the *Indians*, who inhabit near that river, have lately concluded a treaty of peace with the *English;* by which the ancient friendship is renewed with their brethren, and fixed on a firmer foundation than ever. May it be lasting and unmoveable as the mountains. I make no doubt but it gives you equal satisfaction, and that you will unite your endeavours with mine, and all the governors of these provinces, to strengthen it: The clouds, that, for some time, hung over the *English*, and their friends, the *Indians* on the *Ohio*, and kept them both in darkness, are now dispersed, and the chearful light now again shines upon us, and warms us both. May it continue to do so, while the sun and moon give light.

Your people, who were sent to us, were received by us with open arms; they were kindly entertained, while they were here; and I have taken care that they shall return safe to you; with them come trusty messengers, whom I earnestly recommend to your protection; they have several matters in charge; and I desire you may give credit to what they say; in particular, they have a large belt of wampum, and by this belt we let you know, that it is agreed by me, and all the governors, that there shall be an everlasting peace with all the *Indians*, established as sure as the mountains, between the *English* nation and the *Indians*, all over, from the sun rising to the sun setting; and as your influence on them is great, so you will make it known to all the different nations, that want to be in friendship with the *English*; and I hope, by your means and persuasions, many will lay hold on this belt, and immediately withdraw from the *French;* this will be greatly to their own interest and your honor, and I shall not fail to acquaint the great king of it: I sincerely wish it, for their good; for it will fill me with concern, to find any of you joined with the *French;* as in that case, you must be sensible I must treat them as enemies; however, I once more repeat, that there is no time to be lost; for I intend to march with the army very soon; and I hope to enjoy the pleasure of thanking you for your zeal, and of entertaining you in the fort ere long. In the mean time I wish happiness and prosperity to you, your women and children.

I write to you as a warrior should, that is, with candour and love, and I recommend secrecy and dispatch.

> I am, kings *Beaver* and *Shingas*,
>   And brother warriors,
>   Your assured friend and brother,
>   John Forbes.

From my camp at Loyalhannon,
     Nov. 9, 1758.

To Colonel Burd
Shippen papers, p.148

New Camp, 20 miles west of Loyal Hannon,
November 19th, 1758.

Sir:—

> [1]astonished and amazed upon
> and villainous desertion of
> of the methods he had used
> from our assistance at so very critical a time

He has often told us in public

that his nation were going to make war against the Virginians and
His Majesty's subjects. I therefore thought him a good pledge in our
hands to prevent that, and consequently the whole of them were
indulged in every extravagant, avaricious demand they made; but
seeing that those who have thus deserted and abandoned us, with all
the aggravating circumstances attending their desertion, now preludes
to what we may expect from them. I therefore desire, that upon
receipt of this, you will instantly dispatch an express to the commanding officer at Raystown, who is to send one to Winchester and
Fort Cumberland, in case that he, the Carpenter and his followers,
should have already past Raystown, and notice ought to be sent to
Fort Loudon likewise with my orders, which are that having under the
cloak of friendship robbed us these several months, but now having
discovered themselves our private enemies, and having turned the arms,
put in their hands by us, against His Majesty's subjects, which the
former parties have already done, that, therefore prudence and self
preservation obliged us, to require of them the returning of their
arms and ammunition directly, as likewise the horses that were furnished them to accompany us to war; that as their blankets, shirts,
silver truck, &c., are not of that consequence, therefore the peremptory
stripping of them need not
I insist upon the inhabitants[1]
Chester making them do
and horses, which is but
fellow subjects of the parts of Virginia
borough, where no doubt they would commit all sorts of outrage, so
that it will be necessary to send a sufficient escort along with them,
allowing of them a sufficiency of provisions and no more, so that the

[1]Passage lost or indecipherable.

Cherokee nation may see plainly they will have nothing to complain of but the baseness aud perfidy of those, whom they have sent amongst us as friends for these seven months past. The garrison of Fort Cumberland is strong enough to compel them to deliver up their arms, so let a copy of this my letter be sent to the commanding officer, who is to make use of all the fair means in his power before he takes their arms from them. At Raystown they are to do the same.

But as the garrison of Fort Loudon is perhaps too weak either to refuse them their presents, or make them deliver up their arms, I desire, therefore, that in case they take that way, that Major Wells marches directly himself with a sufficient force from Raystown to Fort Loudon to execute this, which you and all concerned, are always first to try by gentle methods, before that rougher ones be made use of; as it is impossible any of your garrison can overtake them before they reach Raystown, I therefore desire no time may be lost in sending copies of my letter and directions to Raystown, to be forthwith transmitted by expresses to Fort Loudon, Cumberland and Winchester. * * * Mr. Smith the interpreter ought to be sent after them to serve to explain matters, and to prevent as far as can be, the bad consequences of their going home through Virginia and North Carolina, armed, for which purpose this letter is wrote, as Virginia has always suffered.

I am, sir,

Your obedient, humble servant,

Jno. Forbes.

Colonel Bouquet to William Allen, Esq., chief justice of Pennsylvania
Rupp's History of western Pennsylvania, apx., p.298

Fort Du Quesne, 25th Nov., 1758.

Dear Sir:—I take, with great pleasure, this first opportunity of informing you of the reduction of this important place, persuaded that the success of his Majesty's arms on this side, will give you a great satisfaction, and reward you for all the pains you have taken for the difficult supply of this army.

We marched from Loyalhanna with 2,500 picked men, without tents or baggage, and a light train of artillery, in the expectation of meeting the enemies, and determining by a battle who should possess this country. The distance is about 50 miles, which we marched in five days, a great diligence, considering the season—the uncertainty of the roads, entirely unknown, and the difficulty of making them practicable for the artillery. The 23d we took post at 12 miles from hence, and halted the 24th for intelligence. In the evening our Indians reported that they had discovered a very thick smoke from the fort, extending in the bottom along the Ohio. A few hours after they sent word that the enemies had abandoned their fort, after having burnt every thing.

We marched this morning and found the report true. They have blown up and destroyed all their fortifications, houses, ovens and magazines—all their Indians' goods burnt in the stores, which seem to have been very considerable.

They seem to have been about 400 men; part is gone down the Ohio, 100 by land, supposed to Presque Isle, and 200 with the Governor, M. de Lignery, to Venango, where he told the Indians he intended to stay this winter, with an intention to dislodge us in the spring. We would soon make him shift his quarters, had we only provisions, but we are scarcely able to maintain ourselves a few days here to treat with the neighboring Indians, who are summoned to meet us. The destruction of the fort, the want of victuals and the impossibility of being supplied in time at this distance and season of the year, obliges us to go back and leave a small detachment of 200 men only, by way of keeping possession of the ground.

This successful expedition can be of great service to the provinces, provided they will improve and support it. It is now the time to take vigorous measures to secure this conquest, and unless Virginia and Pennsylvania can agree upon an immediate assistance, all our pains and advantages will be lost.

An immediate supply of provisions, clothing and necessaries, should at any rate be sent up for the support of the troops, and measures taken for the formation of magazines on the frontiers, (Raystown and Cumberland) for the supply of an army to act early in the spring.

The succors and directions from England would be too late, and if the colonies do not exert themselves to the utmost of their power, I am afraid they will have occasion to repent it.

Indian goods ought to be provided without delay, with a commissary, or proper person to dispose of them, either for trade or presents, as our new friends cannot remain long unprovided, and would soon return to the French were we to leave them in want. Some artificers are also greatly wanted, such as carpenters, smiths, masons, gun-smiths, and chiefly ship builders.

A number of cows and bulls, mares and stallions, garden seeds, corn, &c. Every moment is precious, and the land so rich and the pasture so abundant, that every thing would thrive, and the garrison would soon be able to support itself.

Fish nets and hooks would likewise be of great use for people reduced to salt meat, and some rice, barley, &c., to prevent scurvy among the men.

I enter into all those details with you, because I think the safety of the post depends upon it; and in the plenty you are used to live, they would not so readily occur to you as to us, who are deficient

Sir,

Fort Duquesne
now Pittsbourg 26th November 1758

I have the pleasure and honour of acquainting you with the signal success of his Majesty's troops over all his Enemies on the Ohio, by having obliged them to burn and abandon their Fort Duquesne which they

* * * * * * *

Quaedero

Ship all your hands and flatter myself that if God to Philadelphia, under your care and good Company's I shall of men a good chance of receiving a health that I won the vogue of wining to give your Province all the satisfaction in the power of my weak abilities.

I am Sir,

with great esteem and regard
Your most obedient
humble servant
Jo: Forbes

Governor Denny

of every necessary of life. Could you diffuse into the Assembly the public spirit that directs all your actions, I would be very easy about the consequences. But I know the disposition of the people in general—always indolent, and ready to fall asleep on the smallest gleam of ease and quiet. You must rouse them, and make them sensible that this business is but half done. We have acted our parts, let you do yours. It is now in your power to enjoy in peace and quietness your lands and possessions, if you will only lay out some money, —which may save you ten times more, and the lives of thousands of your poor inhabitants.

After God, the success of this expedition is entirely due to the General, who, by bringing about the treaty with the Indians at Easton, has struck the blow which has knocked the French on the head, in temporizing wisely to expect the effects of that treaty, in securing all his posts, and giving nothing to chance, and not yielding to the urging instances for taking Braddock's road, which would have been our destruction. In all these measures I say he has shown the greatest prudence, firmness and ability. Nobody is better informed of the numberless difficulties he had to surmount than I am, who had an opportunity to see every step that was taken from the beginning, and every obstruction that was thrown in the way. I wish the nation may be as sensible of his service as he really deserves, and give him the reward that can flatter him the pleasure of seeing them pleased and satisfied.

I expect the satisfaction to see you this winter and to talk more at large upon this subject. I beg you will present my compliments to Mrs. Allen, and believe me, with true respect, dear sir,

Henry Boquet.

To Governor Denny
Pennsylvania Colonial records, v.8, p.232

Fort Duquesne, or now Pittsburg, the 26 Nov., 1758.

Sir:

I have the Pleasure and Honour of Acquainting you with the Signal Success of his Majesty's Troops over all his Enemys on the Ohio, by having obliged them to Burn and abandon their Fort, Duquesne, which they effectuated upon the 24th Instant, And of which I took Possession with my little Army the next Day,—The Enemy having made their escape down the River, part in Boats and part by Land, to their Forts, and Settlements on the Mississippi being abandoned, or at least not seconded by their Friends, the Indians, whom we had previously engaged to act a neutral part, And who now seem all willing and ready to Embrace His Majesty's Most gracious Protection.

So give me leave to congratulate you upon this publick event of having totally expelled the French from this Fort and this prodigious tract of Country, and of having in a manner reconciled the various Tribes of Indians inhabiting it to His Majesty's Government.

I have not time to give you a detail of our proceedings and approaches towards the Enemy, or of the Hardships and Difficulties that we necessarily met with; all that will soon come out, but I assure you, after receiving the Ground & Fort, I have great reason to be most thankful for the part that the French have acted.

As the Conquest of this Country is of the greatest Consequence to the adjacent Provinces, by securing the Indians, our real Friends, for their own Advantage, I have therefore sent for their Head People to come to me, when I think in few Words and few Days to make every thing easy; I shall then set out to kiss your Hands, if I have Strength enough left to carry me through the Journey.

I shall be obliged to leave about Two Hundred Men of your Provincial Troops to join a proportion of Virginia and Marylanders, in order to protect this Country during Winter, by which Time I hope the Provinces will be so sensible of the great Benefit of this new Acquisition, as to enable me to fix this noble, fine Country, to all Perpetuity, under the Dominion of Great Britain.

I beg the Barracks may be put in good repair, and proper Lodging for the Officers, and that you will send me, with the greatest Dispatch, your Opinion how I am to dispose of the rest of your Provincial Troops for the ease and Convenience of the Province and the Inhabitants.

You must also remember that Colonel Montgomery's Battalion of Thirteen Hundred Men, and Four Companies of Royal Americans, are, after so long and tedious a Campaign, to be taken care of in some Comfortable Winter Quarters.

I kiss all your Hands, and flatter myself that if I get to Philadelphia, under your Cares and good Companys, I shall yet run a good Chance of re-establishing a Health that I run the risque of ruining to give your Province all the Satisfaction in the Power of my weak Abilities.

I am, Sir, with great Esteem and regard,

Your most Obedient and Hum^e. Servant,

Jo. Forbes.

P. S.—I must beg that you will recommend to your Assembly the building of a Block House and Saw Mill upon the Kisskaminities, near Loyal Hannon, as a thing of the utmost Consequence to their Province, if they have any intention of profiting by this Acquisition.

I send the New Levies to Carlisle, so beg you will loose no time in sending up Mr. Young, the Commissary, to clear them.

View of Pittsburgh, 1796, from Collot's "Voyage dans l'Amerique Septentrionale," engraved by Tardieu

Letter containing account of the defeat of Major Grant
Hazard's Register of Pennsylvania, v.7, p.125

Fort Du Quesne, Nov. 26th, 1758.

Sir,—Our march has been attended with innumerable difficulties, a country wild and desolate, through and across mountains, where civilized man had not before trod, by Indian paths almost impracticable and harrassed at every step by merciless savages who hidden from our view would pour forth their deadly shot with impunity. As we approached the Fort the danger of a surprise became greater; the recollection of the defeat of Braddock made us cautious; I ordered Major Grant who was in the advance to guard against ambuscades.— That officer with three hundred men approached the Fort on the supposition that the French had withdrawn, when suddenly the hostile Indians rose on each side and poured forth a destructive fire and the Garrison numerous and strong rallied out and made a fierce and violent attack; the attack was on every side but Grant ordered a retreat, the men formed a compact band and awed the assailants by a resolute and determined combat. Many were killed, many were taken prisoners, but the success of the enemy met with a powerful check, for they came in contact with the body of the army being led on with skill and circumspection; met them boldly and compelled them to give up their attempts; the retreat of Grant was the last success of the enemy, they were convinced that all hopes of saving the Fort were fruitless; they withdrew to the Fort, destroyed most of the works, and went down the Ohio, in number exceeding five hundred men. On the twenty fourth the English Flag waved triumphantly over Fort Du Quesne. In the third year after the commencement of hostilities about that fortification, it fell into our hands after having kindled so fierce a flame in so destructive a war. With the change of masters it has assumed the name of Fort Pitt, and Pittsburg the propriety of which is too evident to require a justification of the change; two plans of operation have been judicious, extensive, vigorous and successful.

My health is still delicate.

With sentiments of respect

I remain yours, &c.

Forbes.

Captain Haslet to the Rev. Dr. Allison
Rupp's History of western Pennsylvania, apx., p.301

Fort Duquesne, Nov. 26, 1758.

Rev'd Sir:—I have now the pleasure to write you from the ruins of the fort. On the 24th, at night we were informed by one of our Indian scouts, that he had discovered a cloud of smoke above the place, and soon after another came in with certain intelligence that it was burnt and abandoned by the enemy. We were then about 15 miles from it, a troop of horse was sent forward immediately to extinguish the burning, and the whole army followed. We arrived at 6 o'clock last night, and found it in a great measure destroyed. There are two forts about 200 yards distant, the one built with immense labor, small but a great deal of very strong works collected into a little room, and stands on the point of a narrow neck of land at the confluence of the two rivers. It is square and has two ravelins gabions at each corner. The other fort stands on the bank of the Allegheny, in the form of a parallelogram, but not so strong as the other. Several of the out works are lately begun and still unfinished. There are, I think, 30 stacks of chimneys standing—the houses all burnt down. They sprung one mine which ruined one of their magazines. In the other we found 16 barrels of ammunition, a prodigious quantity of old carriage iron, barrels of guns, about a cart load of scalping knives. They went off in such haste they could not quite destroy their works as they intended. We are told by the Indians that they lay the night before last at Beaver creek, 40 miles down the Ohio from here. Whether they buried their dead in the river or carried them down in their batteaux, we have not yet learned. A boy 12 years old who has been their prisoner two years, who escaped on the 2d inst., tells us, they had carried a prodigious quantity of wood into the fort, that they had burnt five of the prisoners that they took at Maj. Grant's defeat, on the parade, and delivered others to the Indians, who were tomahawked on the spot. We have found numbers of dead bodies within a quarter of a mile of the fort unburied, as so many monuments of French humanity! A great many Indians, mostly Delawares, are gathered on the Island last night and this morning, to treat with the General, and we are making rafts to bring them over. Whether the General will think of repairing the ruins or leaving any of the troops here, I have not yet heard. Mr. Beatty is appointed to preach a thanksgiving sermon, for the remarkable superiority of his Majesty's arms. We left all our tents at Loyalhanna, and every convenience except a blanket and knapsack. You will excuse the errors of haste, and believe me to be,

Rev'd sir, your most obedient servant,

John Haslet.

To William Pitt

Correspondence of William Pitt with colonial governors in America, v.1, p.406

Pittsbourgh. 27th Novem^r. 1758.

Sir,

I do myself the Honour of acquainting you that it has pleased God to crown His Majesty's Arms with Success over all His Enemies upon the Ohio, by my having obliged the Enemy to burn and abandon Fort Du Quesne, which they effectuated on the 25th:, and of which I took possession next day, the Enemy having made their Escape down the River towards the Mississippi in their Boats, being abandoned by their Indians, whom I had previously engaged to leave them, and who now seem all willing and ready to implore His Majesty's most Gracious Protection. So give me leave to congratulate you upon this great Event, of having totally expelled the French from this prodigious tract of Country, and of having reconciled the various tribes of Indians inhabiting it to His Majesty's Government.

It would be too tedious for a Letter to enter into the detail how this Affair has been brought to a conclusion, I have therefore thought it proper and necessary to send over to you Brigade Major Halkett whose serving with me all this Campaign, and knowing from whence Events arose will be able to give you a true & succinct Account of the whole Affair from the beginning. I beg to recommend that Gentleman to your Protection, whose Zeal and abilities in the Service have been particularly distinguished, not only in this but in every preceding Campaign from the beginning of the war in this Country, and whose Father Sʳ. Peter Halkett, lost his life at the Monongahela under Genˡ. Braddock.

I should have carried the troops up the River to the Lake Erie, and destroyed the French posts at Venango and Presque Isle, but the Season of the Year, and the Scarcity of my Provisions, does by no Means admitt of it, this last inconveniance (being obliged to carry every bit of my Provisions for Man and horse for betwixt 3 & 400 Miles thro' almost impracticable roads and Mountains) renders it extreamly difficult for me to leave a sufficient Garrison here for the Protection of this Country, as all Manner of Communication with the inhabited parts of the provinces will be cut off during the Winter for at least four Months, notwithstanding that I have built Forts, and erected Posts at proper distances, to have kept the Communication open if possible.

Altho' that I have made frequent Applications not only to the Commander in Chief of His Majesty's Forces for his Orders, and instructions but likewise to the Governours of the adjacent colonies and Provinces for their Advice and Councill how I was to behave myself in case that I was so fortunate as to render myself Master of Fort Du Quesne, and the Country of the Ohio, yet I have never been favoured with any of their Sentiments upon that Subject, except in one letter from the Lieut Governʳ. of Virginia, wherein he tells me that his Assembly and Councill would not venture to give any opinion, but at the same time acquaints me that they had addressed him to recall their troops by the first day of decemʳ., therefore having been left to act intirely from my own judgement hitherto, I must beg His Majesties Indulgence that He would be graciously pleased to attribute my faults or omissions that I may have made, to my want of greater abilities and not to want of Zeal for His Majesty's Service, which I shall ever think my duty to exert to the utmost of my power. As thus you see S^r., that I am without advice or Orders, and that I very soon run a risque of being without troops if Pennsilvania recalled theirs as well as Virginia, I shall soon be greatly difficulted how to maintain our new conquest should the Enemy return, as I will have only 4 Companies of the Royal Americans and Col^o. Montgomery's young Battalion to depend upon, both greatly impaired as to Numbers by their frequent skirmishes with the Enemy during the Campaign.

This far I had wrote at Fort Du Quesne upon the 27th: Novem^r. since which time I have never, either been able to write, or capable to dictate a letter; but as General Amherst acquainted me that he had sent to you my letter with the Accounts of my taking the place, I was the less anxious of sending Major Halkett, but now dreading my silence may have some wrong construction put upon it when the true cause is unknown it will very well bear, I now send you the Major who must give you the best Accounts he can, untill I am able to write more circumstantially, which I hope will be by the first Packett, altho' my Physicians and all our Hospital People unanimously agree that I must go directly for England for to save my life, I must therefore beg it as the greatest favour that you will be so good as to move His Majesty to be graciously pleased to give me His leave of returning home as soon as I possibly can in order to re-establish my health, which at present renders me incapable of any service, or doing any duty whatever.

I must likewise take the boldness, to beg your Countenance & Protection with His Majesty of having me restored to my Rank which is one day antecedent to Genl: Amherst as Lieut. Col^o..—Had I ever committed any fault, or been guilty of any misdeamenor in the Service, I should be now ashamed of making this Application to you, but the having so many people put over my head, without my being sensible of any *faux pas* committed, has made and still makes the deepest impression on my mind. If Lord Ligonier pleases to let you know the hardness of my case, I flatter myself with the protection and Service of M^r. Pitt, to restore me to Peace of mind.

I have used the freedom of giving your name to Fort Du Quesne, as I hope it was in some measure the being actuated by your spirits that now makes us Masters of the place. Nor could I help using the same freedom in the naming of two other Forts that I built (Plans of which I send you) the one Fort Ligonier & the other Bedford. I hope the name Fathers will take them under their Protection, In which case these dreary deserts will soon be the richest and most fertile of any possest by the British in N^o. America. I have the honour to be with great regard and Esteem Sir,

Your most obed^t.. & most hum^le. serv^t.

Jo: Forbes.

Philadelphia. 21st. January 1759.

Colonel Washington to Governor Fauquier
Sparks's Writings of Washington, v.2, p.320

Camp, at Fort Duquesne, 28 November, 1758.

Sir,

I have the pleasure to inform you, that Fort Duquesne, or the ground rather on which it stood, was possessed by his Majesty's troops on the 25th instant. The enemy, after letting us get within a day's march of the place, burned the fort, and ran away by the light of it, at night, going down the Ohio by water, to the number of about five hundred men, according to our best information. This possession of the fort has been matter of surprise to the whole army, and we cannot attribute it to more probable causes, than the weakness of the enemy, want of provisions, and the defection of their Indians. Of these circumstances we were luckily informed by three prisoners, who providentially fell into our hands at Loyal Hanna, when we despaired of proceeding further. A council of war had determined that it was not advisable to advance this season beyond that place; but the above information caused us to march on without tents or baggage, and with only a light train of artillery. We have thus happily succeeded. It would be tedious, and I think unnecessary, to relate every trivial circumstance that has happened since my last. To do this, if needful, shall be the employment of a leisure hour, when I shall have the pleasure to pay my respects to your Honor.

The General intends to wait here a few days to settle matters with the Indians, and then all the troops, except a sufficient garrison to secure the place, will march to their respective governments. I give your Honor this early notice, that your directions relative to the troops of Virginia may meet me on the road. I cannot help reminding you, in this place, of the hardships they have undergone, and of their present naked condition, that you may judge if it is not essential for them to have some little recess from fatigue, and time to provide themselves with necessaries. At present they are destitute of every comfort of life. If I do not get your orders to the contrary, I shall march the troops under my command directly to Winchester. They may then be disposed of as you shall afterwards direct.

General Forbes desires me to inform you, that he is prevented, by a multiplicity of affairs, from writing to you so fully now as he would otherwise have done. He has written to the commanding officers stationed on the communication from hence to Winchester, relative to the conduct of the Little Carpenter, a chief of the Cherokees, the purport of which was to desire, that they would escort him from one place to another, to prevent his doing any mischief to the inhabitants.

This fortunate, and, indeed, unexpected success of our arms will be attended with happy effects. The *Delawares* are suing for peace, and I doubt not that other tribes on the Ohio will follow their ex-ample. A trade, free, open, and on equitable terms, is what they seem much to desire, and I do not know so effectual a way of riveting them to our interest, as by sending out goods immediately to this place for that purpose. It will, at the same time, be a means of supplying the garrison with such necessaries as may be wanted; and, I think, the other colonies, which are as greatly interested in the support of this place as Virginia, should neglect no means in their power to establish and maintain a strong garrison here. Our business, without this precaution, will be but half finished; while, on the other hand, we shall obtain a firm and lasting peace with the Indians, if this end is once accomplished.

General Forbes is very assiduous in getting these matters settled upon a solid basis, and has great merit for the happy issue to which he has brought our affairs, infirm and worn down as he is. At present I have nothing further to add, but the strongest assurances of my being your Honor's most obedient and most humble servant.

George Washington.

LIST OF REFERENCES ON THE EXPEDITION OF GENERAL FORBES AGAINST FORT DUQUESNE.

The call numbers are those of the books in the Carnegie Library of Pittsburgh, and the references are limited to the books in that library.

Albert, George Dallas, *ed.* qr974.881 A33

History of the county of Westmoreland, Pennsylvania. 1882. p.27-31.

Relates somewhat in detail the principal events of the campaign.

Annual Register, 1758. v.1, p.74-75. r905 A61 v.1

Of interest chiefly as a contemporary account.

Avery, Elroy McKendree. q973 A95 v.4

History of the United States. 1904-08. v.4, p.192-213.

The same...qr973 A95 v.4

Interesting and rather full narrative of the campaign. Contains maps, one of them showing the roads of Braddock and Forbes.

Balch, Thomas, *comp.* r974.8 B18

Letters and papers relating chiefly to the provincial history of Pennsylvania. 1855. p.119-152.

These are known as the "Shippen papers." Many of them are letters of Joseph Shippen, brigadier-major to the provincial troops in the campaign, to Forbes, Bouquet and others. There are also included returns of certain of the troops. Valuable contemporary documents.

Bancroft, Aaron. r92 W272b

Life of George Washington. 2v. in 1. 1826. v.1, p.33-39.

Washington's part in the campaign.

Bancroft, George. r973 B22 v.2

History of the United States of America. 1892-93. v.2, p.493-496.

The same...973 B22 v.2

Narrates briefly the chief events and the results of the campaign.

Banvard, Joseph. 973.1 B22p

Pioneers of the New World and the old French war. 1880. p.196-208.

Good popular account.

Boucher, John Newton. qr974.886 B65 v.1

A century and a half of Pittsburg and her people. 1908. v.1, p.27-42.

The same...q974.886 B65 v.1

The Forbes campaign.

Includes map showing route from Laurel Ridge.

Boucher, John Newton.   **qr974.881 B65. v.1**

History of Westmoreland County, Pennsylvania. 1906. v.1, p.13-24.

Interesting account of the campaign, including a number of details not usually given. Contains a map of the county showing that part of Forbes's route.

Bradley, Arthur Granville.   **973.2 B68**

The fight with France for North America. [1901.] p.268-287.

Relates with some fulness the plans and events of the campaign.

"The narrative is so consecutive, so little encumbered with unimportant detail, that the whole remains clear and distinct. . . . He has a knowledge of conditions and localities which saves him happily from those misconceptions and errors irritating to . . . those who have inherited the land and its traditions."   *Larned's Literature of American history.*

Brady, Cyrus Townsend.   **973.2 B686**

Colonial fights and fighters. 1901. p.243-260.

Popular narrative of the campaign, including Grant's defeat.

Browne, James.   **941 B81 v.4**

History of the Highlands and of the Highland clans. 1854. v.4, p.244-246.

The part taken in the campaign by the 1,200 Scotch Highlanders of Montgomery's regiment. List of officers is included.

Chapman, Thomas Jefferson.   **r974.88 C36**

The French in the Allegheny valley. 1887. p.87-99, 158-186.

The same..974.88 C36

The fall of Fort Duquesne.—Post's first visit to the western Indians.—Post's second mission.

"The fall of Fort Duquesne" appeared also in Magazine of American History," April 1887, v.17, p.330-335 (r973 M24 v.17).

"Not a contribution to knowledge, but it may be commended as a contribution to popular information." *Larned's Literature of American history.*

Church, Samuel Harden.   **r974.886 C46**

Short history of Pittsburgh, 1758-1908. 1908. p.27-30.

The same..974.886 C46

Brief account.

Colonial Dames of America, Society of.   **973.3 C72 v.2-3**

Letters to Washington, and accompanying papers; ed. by S. M. Hamilton. 1898-1902. v.2, p.254-410; v.3, p.1-150.

Letters of 1758. Many of the letters of this year, especially those of the second half, were written to Washington as commander of the Virginia troops by Col. Bouquet, Lieut.-Col. Stephen and others prominent in the campaign.

Craig, Neville B.   **r974.886 C86**

History of Pittsburgh. 1851. p.71-79.

The same..974.886 C86

Brief history of the campaign, quoting the account from the "Pennsylvania Gazette" and a statement by Commissary Ormsby. Includes also the return of Forbes's army on Sept. 25, 1758.

Dahlinger, Charles William.   **r974.886 D15**
1758; being a sketch of the founding of Pittsburgh. 1908.
The same..**974.886 D15**
<small>Reprinted from the Pittsburgh Gazette-Times, Sept. 27, 1908.</small>

Darlington, *Mrs.* Mary Carson (O'Hara), *comp.*   **qr974.886 D25**
Fort Pitt and letters from the frontier. 1892. p.63-83.
The same..**q974.886 D25**
<small>Maj. Grant's letter to Gen. Forbes upon the affair of Sept. 14, 1758.—Letter of
Gen. Forbes to Col. Bouquet, Raestown, Sept. 23, 1758.—Letter of Col. Bouquet to
Gen. Forbes, Loyal Hanna, Sept. 17, 1758.—Letter of Col. Burd to Col. Bouquet,
Loyal Hannon, Oct. 12, 1758.—Letter of Col. Bouquet [to Gen. Forbes], Oct. 13, 1758.
  Chiefly from the Bouquet papers in the British Museum. The first three letters
are especially interesting: Grant's account to his general, of his defeat; Forbes's long
letter on the roads, and details of the campaign; Bouquet's official letter to Forbes
describing and explaining Grant's defeat.</small>

Darlington, *Mrs.* Mary Carson (O'Hara), *ed.*   **r92 B655d**
History of Colonel Henry Bouquet and the western frontiers of
Pennsylvania, 1747-64. 1920. p.92-101.
<small>The Forbes expedition.</small>

Daughters of the American Revolution,   **r974.886 D28**
      Pittsburgh Chapter.
Fort Duquesne and Fort Pitt. 1899. p.16-22.
The same..**974.886 D28**
<small>Brief popular account, based on Parkman.</small>

                                                              r920 S82d v.2
Dictionary of national biography; supplement. 1901. v.2, p.223-224.
<small>Short sketch of Gen. Forbes, by Col. E. M. Lloyd.</small>

Donehoo, George P. *ed.*   **qr974.8 D72p v.2**
Pennsylvania; a history. 1926. v.2, p.814-837.
The same..**q974.8 D72p v.2**
<small>The expedition of General John Forbes against Fort Duquesne in 1758.</small>

Doyle, John Andrew.   **973.2 D77 v.5**
English colonies in America. 1889-1907. v.5, p.477-480.
<small>Condensed account based on the best authorities.</small>

Entick, John.   **r943 E66 v.3**
General history of the late war. 1763-65. v.3, p.262-267.
<small>Contemporary account of the campaign, brief, but told with vigor by one to
whom the events were still freshly in mind.</small>

Everts, (L. H.) & Co. *pub.*   **qr974.885 E95**
History of Allegheny Co., Pennsylvania. 1876. p.34-37.
<small>Relates somewhat in detail the events of the campaign.</small>

Fiske, John.   **973.2 F54n**
New France and New England. 1902. p.336-342.
<small>Brief account of the campaign as one of the decisive events in the fall of France
in North America.</small>

Fleming, George Thornton, *and others.*   qr974.886 F62 v.1
History of Pittsburgh and environs. 1922. v.1, p.385-416.
The same...q974.886 F62 v.1
Two chapters:
John Forbes and General Grant.—"I have called the place Pittsburgh."

Forbes, *Gen.* John.   r016.9748 C21e
Letters relating to the expedition against Fort Duquesne. 1909.
Assembled from numerous sources.
Appeared in Monthly Bulletin of the Carnegie Library of Pittsburgh Feb.-May,
1909. Now out of print. These letters, with additions, are reproduced in the present
collection.

Ford, Worthington Chauncey.   qr92 W272fo v.1
George Washington. 1900. v.1, p.93-106.
Although primarily on Washington's part in the campaign, gives a rather full
account of the expedition as a whole.

Fort Duquesne.   qr974.886 F79
Baptismal register of Fort Duquesne; tr. by A. A. Lambing. 1885.
p.25-27.
Very brief account of the campaign, with contemporary descriptions of the fort
by John McKinney, held prisoner there, and Capt. Haslet, one of Forbes's officers.

Fortescue, John William.   354.42 F79 v.2
History of the British army. 1899-1902. v.2, p.333-338.
Excellent short account of the campaign, from the military point of view.

Hazard, Samuel, *ed.*   qr974.8 H37 v.6
Register of Pennsylvania. October 9, 1830. v.6, p.226-227.
Letter from Col. Bouquet to William Allen, chief justice of Pennsylvania, dated
Fort Duquesne, Nov. 25, 1758, describing the capture of the fort; also a letter on the
same subject from Capt. Haslet to the Rev. Dr. Alison, dated Fort Duquesne, Nov.
26, 1758.

Hazard, Samuel, *ed.*   qr974.8 H37 v.8
Register of Pennsylvania. August 27, 1831. v.8, p.141.
Letter dated Annapolis, Oct. 5, 1758, describing Grant's defeat; published in the
"Pennsylvania Gazette" of Oct. 12, 1758.

Hazard, Samuel, *ed.*   qr974.8 H37 v.11
Register of Pennsylvania. June 29, 1833. v.11, p.414.
Account of the capture of Fort Duquesne, from the "Pittsburg Gazette."

Hulbert, Archer Butler, *comp.*   qr912.7 H91 v.2
Crown collection of photographs of American maps. v.2, no.22;
Plan of Fort Du Quesne such as it was before it was demolished, 1758,
by J. C. Pleydell.

Hulbert, Archer Butler.   r973 H91 v.5
The Old Glade (Forbes's) road (Pennsylvania state road). 1903.
(Historic highways of America, v.5.)
The same...973 H91 v.5
This history of Forbes's road forms also a valuable and interesting history of the
campaign for which the road was built. The controversy that arose between Vir-
ginia and Pennsylvania when Forbes, abandoning his original plan of marching by
Braddock's road, decided to open a new and more direct road to the Ohio, is discussed

with especial fulness. The author has taken his material from the original sources;
the correspondence of Forbes, Bouquet and St. Clair preserved in the British Museum and in the British Public Record Office.
   Map of Forbes's road, to Raystown, p.108.

Irving, Washington.   **92W272i v.1**
   Life of George Washington. [1856-57.] v.1, p.323-339.
   "Tells the story of Forbes's campaign. . . . A graceful rendering of accessible
knowledge, with but little independent research of importance." *Winsor's Narrative and
critical history of America.*

Jenkins, Howard M. *ed.*   **qr974.8 J25 v.1**
   Pennsylvania, colonial and federal. 1903. v.1, p.483-498.
   The same..q974.8 J25p v.1
   Relates with some fulness the preparations for the campaign, the actions of the
Assembly, negotiations with the Indians, controversy over the choice of route, with
brief account of the successful close of the expedition.

Johnson, Rossiter.   **973.2 J36**
   History of the French war ending in the conquest of Canada. 1882.
p.294-301.
   Brief popular narrative.

Killikelly, Sarah Howe.   **r974.886 K25**
   History of Pittsburgh. 1906. p.28-35.
   The same..974.886 K25
   Brief account, consisting chiefly of the letter from Capt. Haslet to the Rev. Dr.
Allison, and two other contemporary letters on the campaign, all of which appeared
in the Rhode Island "Mercury" of Dec. 1758. Washington's letter to Gov. Fauquier,
announcing the capture of the fort is also included.

Kingsford, William.   **r971 K27 v.4**
   History of Canada. 1890. v.4, p.191-216.
   One of the most interesting, detailed and trustworthy accounts of the campaign,
including full description of Grant's defeat. The character and personality of Forbes
are excellently portrayed, his skill as a general, his determination, his sense of
justice and his recognition of faithful work on the part of his officers and men. The
road controversy is fully discussed, with map (opp. p.196) showing both Braddock's and Forbes's roads. On p.215 may be found the description by Lieut. James
Grant of a medal which Forbes designed and intended to have made and presented
to his officers in the campaign.
   A few extracts from Forbes's letters are included.

Lossing, Benson John.   **qr92 W272los v.1**
   Washington and the American republic. [1870.] v.1, p.269-285.
   History of the campaign, especially Washington's services.

Lowdermilk, Will H.   **r975.2 L95**
   History of Cumberland (Maryland). 1878. p.231-252.
   In this account of the campaign Washington's part is made especially prominent. He opposed Forbes's plan to cut a new road to Fort Duquesne, and part of
his correspondence with Bouquet, who upheld the plan, is here included.

Maclean, John Patterson.   **r973.2 M19**
   Historical account of the settlements of Scotch Highlanders in
America prior to the peace of 1783. 1900. p.265-268.
   On the part taken in the campaign by the 1,200 Highlanders of Montgomery's
regiment.

McSherry, James.　　　　　　　　　　　　　　　　r975.2 M22
　　History of Maryland.　1849.　p.145-149.
　　The services of Maryland in the campaign.

Maps—Pennsylvania.　1758.　　　　　　　　　　qr912.748 M27
　　General Forbes marching journal to the Ohio [made by John Potts].
　　Photostat from the original in the library of the Pennsylvania Historical Society, Philadelphia.

Marshall, John.　　　　　　　　　　　　　　　　r92 W272m v.1
　　Life of George Washington.　1832.　v.1, p.22-26.
　　The same.　1804-07.　v.2, p.55-70...............................r92 W272m1 v.2
　　Short account of the campaign, with special reference to Washington's connection with it.

Maryland—General assembly.　　　　　　　　　　qr328.75 M43 v.9
　　Archives of Maryland.　1883-1907.　v.9:　Correspondence of Gov. Horatio Sharpe, v.2, p.124-321.
　　The letters for the year 1758, including many to and from Gov. Sharpe, Gov. Denny of Pennsylvania, Forbes, St. Clair and others, not only show Maryland's part in the campaign, but also bring out circumstances and details which are of interest in connection with the campaign as a whole.　The difficulties under which the governors worked in trying to induce the legislatures to grant money and troops are clearly shown; many of the preparations for the march, the movements of troops, the hardships endured may be followed in detail, and the uncertainty, at that time, of the outcome be more fully realized.

Parkman, Francis.　　　　　　　　　　　　　　　r973.2 P24m v.2
　　Montcalm and Wolfe.　1897-98.　v.2, p.339-372.
　　The same.　1894-98.　v.2, p.131-163........................973.2 P24m v.2
　　The most satisfactory and interesting general account of the campaign, based upon the original authorities and giving the sources of information.　The author had copies of the official correspondence of Forbes, Bouquet and others relating to the campaign, and quotes frequently from their letters.

Patterson, A. W.　　　　　　　　　　　　　　　　r975.5 P31
　　History of the backwoods.　1843.　p.105-117.
　　Relates with some fulness the events of the campaign, including Grant's defeat.

Patterson, Burd Shippen.　　　　　　　　　　　　rP312h
　　"The Head of Iron"; a romance of colonial Pennsylvania.　1908.
　　The same P312h
　　The theme is the struggle for the possession of the Forks of the Ohio.

Pennsylvania—Commission on frontier forts.　　qr974.8 P3998 v.2
　　Report.　1896.　v.2, p.78-99.
　　The same...q974.8 P3992 v.2
　　Excellent account, chiefly from the military point of view.　Founded on original sources, some of which are quoted with considerable fulness.　Among these are Grant's detailed letter to Forbes giving his own story of his defeat, extracts from French archives on the same subject, and on the actual condition of the fort immediately before its abandonment.　The letter of Capt. Haslet to the Rev. Dr. Allison is also included.

Pennsylvania—General assembly.   r974.8 P399p v.3
   Pennsylvania archives, 1st series. 1852-56. v.3, p.325-574.
   Covering the year 1758. Some of the letters, records and documents relate to the
campaign, among them being the report of Charles Thomson and Frederick Post on
their journey among the Indians, Post's first journal, and letters from officers and
others showing progress of the campaign.

Pennsylvania—General assembly.   r974.8 P399p1 v.6
   Pennsylvania archives, 2nd series. 1875-90. v.6, p.418-419, 422-433.
   Official correspondence relating to Fort Duquesne in 1758, chiefly by French officers. It shows their knowledge of the movements of Forbes's army, also their great
doubt as to their ability to hold Fort Duquesne against the English. Short accounts
of Grant's defeat, both from the French and the English side, are also included.

Pennsylvania—General assembly.   qr328.74 P39v v.5
   Votes and proceedings of the House of representatives of the province of Pennsylvania, Oct. 14, 1758-Sept. 26, 1767. 1775. v.5, p.2-4,
10-12.
   Speech of Gov. Denny to the Assembly, Nov. 16, 1758, on the state of the campaign, with letter of Forbes on the same subject, also message of the governor to the
Assembly and letter of Forbes from Fort Duquesne announcing the success of the
campaign.

Pennsylvania—Provincial council.   r974.8 P3999 v.8
   Minutes. 1851-60. v.8, p.1-241.
   Known as "Colonial records." The minutes of 1758, included in these pages con-
tain many records relating to the campaign; messages of the Assembly and the
governor on preparations, voting of troops and supplies, and reports on Indian con-
ferences.

Pennsylvania-German Society.   r974.8 P3993 v.15
   Proceedings and addresses. 1906. v.15, p.489-508.
   Part of H. M. M. Richards's "Pennsylvania-German in the French and Indian
War."
   The Royal American regiment consisted chiefly of Pennsylvania Germans under
the command of German-speaking officers. One battalion was commanded by Col.
Bouquet and did excellent service in the campaign. A short account of the regiment
and of the campaign as a whole is given here.

Pitt, William.   973.2 P67 v.1
   Correspondence when secretary of state with colonial governors
and military and naval commissioners in America. 1906. v.1, p.41-46.
   Short account of the campaign, by the editor, G. S. Kimball, with quotations from
letters of Forbes.

Post, Christian Frederick.   r917.8 T43 v.1
   Journals. July 15-Sept. 20, 1758; Oct. 25, 1758-Jan. 10, 1759. (In
Thwaites, R. G. *ed.* Early Western travels. 1904-07. v.1, p.175-291.)
   The same..917.7 T43e
   The same. (In Proud, Robert. History of Pennsylvania. 1797-98.
v.2, apx. p.65-132.)..r974.8 P97 v.2
   The same. (In Rupp, I. D. Early history of western Pennsyl-
vania. 1846. apx. p.75-126.)..r974.88 R88
   The same. (In Olden Time. March-April 1846. v.1, p.99-125, 145-
177.)..r974.88 O23 v.1

The same, first journal and extracts from second. (In Pennsylvania archives, 1st ser. v.3, p.520-544, 560-565.)........r974.8 **P399p v.3**

The same, second journal. (In Caldwell, J. A. *pub.* History of Indiana County, Penn'a. 1880. p.83-95.)..............................qr974.889 C13

The withdrawal of the Indians from the French interests was of great importance to the success of Forbes's campaign. The great danger to the army was that it might be attacked and routed in the march by the Indians. To prevent this a proper person was sought who would venture among those hostile Indians with a message. The person selected was Christian Frederick Post, a plain, honest, religiously disposed man, who, from a conscientious opinion of duty, formerly went among the Indians to convert them to Christianity. He married twice among them and lived with them for 17 years, attaining a full knowledge of their language and customs. Both his wives being dead, he returned to live among the white people, but at the request of the governor readily undertook this hazardous journey. How he executed his trust his "Journal" will show. *Condensed from Thomson's introduction to the Journal.*

"Sufficient credit has not been given to this mission of peace. . . . A careful reading of Posts's second journal . . . shows clearly . . . that the Indians changed their allegiance from the French to the British (in spite of every opposition on the part of the French officers), because of the message Post carried to them." *Spears & Clark's History of the Mississippi valley.*

Pouchot.   **qr973.2 P86 v.1**

Memoir upon the late war in North America. 1866. v.1, p.128-132.

Brief contemporary account, from the French point of view. Pouchot was captain in a French battalion sent out to oppose the English in Canada.

Ritenour, John S.   **r974.88 R51**

Old Tom Fossit. 1926. p.152-166.

The same..974.88 R51

A sick general's triumph.

Brief account of the campaign. Includes a picture of the family home of Gen. Forbes, Pittencrieff, Scotland.

Rupp, Israel Daniel.   **r974.88 R88**

Early history of western Pennsylvania. 1846. p.131-143, apx. p. 298-303.

Full and trustworthy history of the campaign, including Grant's defeat. Contains many references to authorities, and letter from Forbes to Gov. Denny, March 20, 1758, in regard to troops to be raised in Pennsylvania. In the appendix are included letters written at the site of Fort Duquesne, Nov. 25-28, 1758, by Forbes, Bouquet, Washington and John Haslet, describing the capture of the fort.

Sargent, Winthrop.   **r974.8 P39 v.5**

History of an expedition against Fort Du Quesne in 1755 under Maj.-Gen. Edward Braddock. 1855. p.270-278. (In Pennsylvania Historical Society. Publications, v.5.)

The same..974.886 S24

On the latter part of the campaign of 1758 and the entry of the English into the evacuated fort.

Schroeder, John Frederick.   **qr92 W272sc**

Life and times of Washington. [1857.] v.1, p.105-122.

Detailed narrative of Washington's part in the campaign, forming also a good general account of the expedition as a whole.

Smith, James.   r970.1 S65
Account of the remarkable occurrences during his captivity with
the Indians. 1870. p.102-105.
The same. (In Drake, S. G. Indian captivities. 1853.
p.233-234 ....r970.1 D78
   Col. Smith was a Pennsylvanian who had been held captive by the Indians since
the time of Braddock's expedition. At the time of Forbes's campaign he was at
Detroit, where he was able to learn from the Indians what he here briefly relates of
the progress and success of Forbes's army and of Grant's defeat. Parkman speaks of
his book as "perhaps the best of all the numerous narratives of the captives among
the Indians."

Sparks, Jared.   r308 W27s v.1
Life of George Washington. 1837. v.1, p.90-102.
The same. p.80-92............................ ....92 W272s
   Short general account of the campaign, with especial reference to Washington's
services.

Volwiler, Albert Tangeman.   r974.8 V37
George Croghan and the westward movement, 1741-1782. 1926.
p.136-142.
The same..974.8 V37

Walton, Joseph Solomon.   r974.8 W19c
Conrad Weiser and the Indian policy of colonial Pennsylvania.
1900. p.360-380.
The same..974.8 W19
   Weiser, a German in the service of the province of Pennsylvania, was the cham-
pion of the English among the Indians. Discusses the relations of the Indians with
the English and French at the time of the campaign and describes the work of Post,
the Moravian missionary who brought about the withdrawal of the Indians from the
French.

Warner, (A) & Co. *pub.*   qr974.885 W23 v.1
History of Allegheny County, Pennsylvania. 1889. v.1, p.41-44.
   Relates briefly the chief events of the campaign.

Washington, George.   r308 W27 v.2
Writings; ed. by W. C. Ford. 1889-93. v.2, p.1-125.
   Letters of 1758 relating chiefly to Forbes's expedition and the fall of Fort Du-
quesne.
The same; ed. by Jared Sparks. 1834-37. v.2,
p.271-327..r308 W27s v.2
   Contains substantially the same letters as those in Ford's edition, but omits a num-
ber of the Bouquet letters. Opposite page 38 is a map on which are traced both Braddock's road and Forbes's road.
   As commander of the Virginia troops in the expedition against Fort Duquesne
Washington took a prominent part in the campaign, his military ability and his experience under Braddock three years before making his services especially valuable
As to the choice of route to the fort he disagreed with Forbes, whose confidence it i:
evident he did not entirely possess, and who considered that Washington's "be-
havior about the roads was noways like a soldier." Although the decision was mad
against him and in favor of a plan which he believed would end in defeat, hi:
services were given none the less freely on this account; and as Parkman says in hi:
chapter on Fort Duquesne, "nobody can read the letters of Washington at this tim
without feeling that the imputations of Forbes were unjust, and that here as else
where, his ruling motive was the public good."

Washington, George.   **qr92 W272mo**
 Monuments of Washington's patriotism. 1841. 4 pp. (inserted be-
fore p.65).
 Letter in answer to a request from Gen. Forbes, with two plans, all in facsimile.
It expresses Washington's "Thoughts on a Line of March" representing "first a Line
of March and secondly how that Line of March may in an Instant be thrown into an
Order of Battle in the Woods."
 A portion of the plan, not in facsimile, may be seen in Sparks's edition of Wash-
ington's writings, v.2, opp. p.314 (r308 W27s v.2).

Whitehead, Cortlandt, bp.   **r974.886 W63**
 Capture of Fort Duquesne; an historical discourse before the Society of Colonial Wars in the Commonwealth of Pennsylvania, delivered in Christ Church, Nov. 27, 1898, upon the occasion of the un-
veiling of a memorial tablet of Brigadier-General John Forbes.

Winsor, Justin.   **977 W79**
 Mississippi basin. 1895. p.386-394.
 Relates the events of the campaign briefly and accurately.

Winsor, Justin, ed.   **r970 W79 v.5**
 Narrative and critical history of America. 1884-89. v.5, p.528-
530, 599.
 Condensed account of the campaign, based on original authorities, the references
to which, as here given, form a valuable bibliography of the subject.

MAGAZINE ARTICLES

Americana. July 1922. v. 16, p.199-233.   **qr973 A5123 v.16**
 "I have called the place Pittsburgh", by G. T. Fleming.
 Condensed from his "History of Pittsburgh and environs." Includes picture of
Pittsburgh in 1790.

                                                             r052 G29 v.29
Gentleman's Magazine. Jan., April 1759. v.29, p.39, 171-174.
 Letter from an officer who attended Forbes, dated Fort Duquesne, Feb. 25, 1759
and describing concisely the military arrangements for the campaign and more in
detail the circumstances of the march and the capture of the fort.

Olden Time. April 1846. v.1, p.177-185.   **r974.88 O23 v.1**
 Historical incidents connected with the capture of Fort Duquesne. Contemporary
Accounts: letter from Col. Bouquet to William Allen, chief justice of Pennsylvania;
letter from Capt. Haslet to the Rev. Dr. Alison; account taken from the "Pittsburgh
Gazette"; letter first published in the "Pennsylvania Gazette" containing a full account
of Grant's defeat; extract from a letter describing an attack of the French and
Indians upon the English forces on Oct. 12.

Olden Time. April 1846. v.1, p.189-190.   **r974.88 O23 v.1**
 Notice of the death of Gen. Forbes, with sketch of his life and character, taken
from the "Pennsylvania Gazette," March 15, 1759.

                                                             r974.88 O23 v.1
Olden Time. June 1846. v.1, p.262-268, 281-283, 285-286.
 On the controversy as to the best route to Fort Duquesne, with letter of Washington Aug. 2, 1758, in favor of the southern route.—Letter of Washington to Gov.
Fauquier of Virginia describing the capture of the fort.—Letter from Robert Munford
to Theodorick Bland showing "the temper of the Virginians in relation to the proposed road from Raystown to Fort Duquesne."

Olden Time. January 1847. v.2, p.2-3. r974.88 O23 v.2

Part of the narrative of John Ormsby, who, as commissary of provisions, accompanied Forbes on the campaign. He became later a well-known resident of Pittsburgh. This extract from his own short sketch of his life describes briefly the capture of the fort, but its interest lies chiefly in the vivid picture of hardships during and following the campaign.

Olden Time. June 1847. v.2, p.283-284. r974.88 O23 v.2

The names of officers killed or missing, taken prisoner, and returned with number of soldiers killed or missing, at Grant's defeat. Also number of officers and soldiers under Gen. Forbes at Raystown, Sept. 25, 1758.

Pennsylvania Magazine. 1887. v.11, p.120-121. qr974.8 P3992 v.11

Obituary notice of Gen. Forbes, from the "Pennsylvania Gazette," March 15, 1759. Short sketch of his life and character, with the order of march at his funeral.

Pennsylvania Magazine. 1888. v.12, p.433-434. qr974.8 P3992 v.12

Extract from the diary of Hannah Callender of Philadelphia, for 1758, in which she notes the "news of Fort Duquesne being forsaken by the French," the burial of the remains of Braddock's men, and the naming of Pittsburgh.

qr974.8 P3992 v.32-33

Pennsylvania Magazine. 1908-1909. v.32, p.433-458; v.33, p. 102-117, 216-227.

Selections from the military correspondence of Colonel Henry Bouquet, 1757-1764.

Letters relating to the Forbes expedition.

Pennsylvania Magazine. 1909. v.33, p.86-98. qr974.8 P3992 v.33

Letters of Gen. John Forbes, 1758.

Pennsylvania Magazine. 1913. v.37, p.395-449. qr974.8 P3992 v.37

James Kenny's "Journal to ye westward", 1758-1759, edited by J. W. Jordan.

Describes his journey to Pittsburgh via York, Frederick, Cumberland and Braddock's road, and his residence at Pittsburgh which, following closely on the expedition against Fort Duquesne under Gen. Forbes is of interest.

NEWSPAPER ARTICLES

These may be seen in the regular files of the papers or in the collection of mounted newspaper clippings kept at the reference desk.

Pittsburgh Gazette. December 1, 1901.

Short article on Forbes, his family and the Forbes estate, Pittencrieff, in Dunfermline, Scotland.

Pittsburgh Gazette. December 8, 1901.

Career of Forbes as an officer in the Scots Greys.

Pittsburgh Gazette. March 8, 1903.

The trail of Forbes's army through Pittsburgh. Describes the route in detail, with map and illustrations.

This article and the one following are founded on notes taken down by Maj. Ebenezer Denny from the account given to him by Capt. Perchmont, who served in the campaign and later owned the land back of Wilkinsburg on which the army camped just before entering the fort.

Pittsburg Leader. December 9, 1900.

The route of Forbes's army in 1758; detailed description, with map.

CENTENNIAL CELEBRATION OF THE EVACUATION OF FORT DUQUESNE, 1858

Denny, William Henry.   r811 D43

Suc-co-tash [a poem]; written on the occasion of the centennial celebration of the evacuation of Fort Duquesne. 1858.

"These lines were written at the request of the Proprietor and Lessees of the Pittsburgh Theater, a few days before the Centennial Celebration, and were read by the stage manager, on that occasion." *Author's note.*

Loomis, A. W.   r974.886 L85

Oration delivered at the centennial celebration of the evacuation of Fort Duquesne, Pittsburgh, November 25, 1858. 1859.

Der Freiheits-Freund.   November 27, 1858.

Account of the celebration.

Pittsburg Dispatch.   November 25, 26, 1858.

Fort Du Quesne; a historical ballad, by Florus B. Plimpton.—The centennial anniversary; description of procession, letters, synopsis of Mr. Loomis's oration, ode "One hundred years ago."

Pittsburgh Evening Chronicle.   November 25, 1858.

Nearly half of this account of the celebration consists of a historical sketch of Pittsburgh to about 1776. Includes a historical ballad describing the capture of the fort, F. B. Plimpton's poem, description of the procession, and congratulatory letters from prominent public men.

Pittsburgh Gazette.   November 25, 1858.

Stanzas commemorative of the occasion, by Robert P. Nevin.

Pittsburg Post.   November 26, 1858.

Full description of the celebration.

SESQUICENTENNIAL CELEBRATION, 1908

The Carnegie Library of Pittsburgh has preserved all the printed accounts of the celebration—the special editions of the newspapers devoted to the subject, the official programmes and history, and a number of other publications, which appeared at that time.

BIBLIOGRAPHY

See also the second entry under Winsor.

Carnegie Library of Pittsburgh.   r016.9748 C21e

Expedition of General Forbes against Fort Duquesne; references to books and magazines articles. 1908.

Reprinted from the Monthly Bulletin, June, 1908.

Carnegie Library of Pittsburgh.   r016.9748 C21

Pennsylvania, a reading list for the use of schools. 1911. p.27-31.

Fall of Fort Duquesne and the building of Fort Pitt.

Committee on Historical Research

Mrs. Sumner Boyer Ely, *Chairman.*

Mrs. Marcellin Cote Adams.

Miss Sarah E. Bissell.

Mrs. Charles W. Dahlinger.

Mrs. G. Cook Kimball.

Mrs. Alexander Laughlin, Jr.

Mrs. Telesio Lucci.

Mrs. James R. Macfarlane.

Lightning Source UK Ltd.
Milton Keynes UK
UKHW041321120220
358590UK00009B/11